EARLY   IETY

XINRU LIU

Early Buddhist Society

The World of Gautama Buddha

SUNY PRESS

First published by Permanent Black D-28 Oxford Apts, 11 IP Extension, Delhi 110092 INDIA, for the territory of SOUTH ASIA. First SUNY Press edition 2022. Not for sale in South Asia.

Published by State University of New York Press, Albany

Cover design by Anuradha Roy

© 2022 Xinru Liu

All rights reserved

Printed in the United States of America

No part of this book may be used or reproduced in any manner whatsoever without written permission. No part of this book may be stored in a retrieval system or transmitted in any form or by any means including electronic, electrostatic, magnetic tape, mechanical, photocopying, recording, or otherwise without the prior permission in writing of the publisher.

For information, contact State University of New York Press, Albany, NY
www.sunypress.edu

Library of Congress Cataloging-in-Publication Data

Names: Liu, Xinru, author
Title: Early Buddhist society : the world of Gautama Buddha
Description: Albany : State University of New York Press, [2022] | Includes bibliographical references and index.
Identifiers: ISBN 9781438491233 (hardcover : alk. paper) | ISBN 9781438491240 (e-book) | ISBN 9781438491226 (paperback)
Further information is available at the Library of Congress.

10 9 8 7 6 5 4 3 2 1

Contents

	Preface and Acknowledgements	ix
	Glossary	xiii
1	The Time of the Buddha	1
2	Ahura and Asura: Persians and Indians in the Time of the Buddha	26
3	The Maladies of Urban Life: Epidemics, Asava, and the Problem of Addiction	50
4	Supporters in the Cities: Gahapati, Setthi, Visakha, and Women Who Fed the Sangha	71
5	Bimbisara, Pasenadi, Ajatasattu, and the Vajji Rajas	94
6	Queens and the Buddhist Sangha	116
7	Patacara and Refugees Who Fled from Cities	138
8	Newcomers from Forests, Mountains, and Waters	148
9	From Aryans to Candalas: A Mobile Hierarchy in the Buddhist Universe	162
10	Sanchi and Bharhut: Visual Memories of Early Buddhist Society	180
	Bibliography	196
	Index	203

Illustrations

1	Sanchi Stupa 1, eastern torana, south pillar, north face	43

2	A member of Delegation VI, Lydians, on the east side of the Apadana Palace at Persepolis	44
3	Sanchi Stupa 1, foreigners worshipping a stupa	45
4	Sassanid motif relief on Sanchi Stupa 2, ground balustrade, north entrance panel on pillar	46
5	Bharhut Stupa, Persian patron	47
6	Sirima Devata, Bharhut Stupa	87
7	Orchestra and dancing in the heavens	88
8	Ajatasattu worshipping the lord. The Buddha is represented here by a pair of sandals	105
9	Women worshipping the Buddha, Amaravati Stupa	143
10	The inscription reads: "Vedisa Chapadevaya Revatimita Bhariyaya pathama danam"	157
11	Suchiloma Yakkho, great railing of Bharhut Stupa	159
12	Celebrating the enlightenment of the Buddha	160
13	The realm of the gods, Bharhut Stupa	165
14	Kubera Yakkho	166
15	Sanchi: Ashoka and the Naga king worship the Buddha	173
16	Bharhut: Aya Isidinasa Bhanakasa (reciter) danam. Erapato Nagaraja Bhagavato Vadate	176
17	Sanchi: Nagaraja Mucilinda	177
18	Sujata feeds a dead ox, Bharhut	179
19	Stupa 1, Sanchi, general view from the south-east	182
20	Sanchi Stupa 1, southern gate, east face of left pillar, showing Ashoka's visit to Bodhgaya and worship of the hair and turban of the Buddha	183
21	Bimbisara, king of Magadha, going out of the city of Rajagaha, Sanchi Stupa 1, northern gate, east pillar of west face	184

22	Royal procession of Pasenadi going out of the city of Savatthi, Sanchi Stupa 1, northern gate, north side of the east pillar	185
23	Battle for the relics of the Buddha, Sanchi Stupa 1, southern gate, north face of lower beam	186
24	Bharhut Stupa, great railing	187
25	Devata Culacoka, great railing, Bharhut Stupa	188
26	Cada Yakkhi, Bharhut Stupa, great railing	189
27	Virudhaka Yakkho, Bharhut great railing pillar,	190
28	Gangito Yakkho, great railing pillar	191
29	Cakavako Nagaraja	192
30	Mahakapi Jataka, great railing, pillar	193
31a and 31b	Monkeys capturing elephant, Bharhut Stupa, great railing crossbar	194

Preface
and Acknowledgements

FORTY YEARS AGO, when I studied early India with Romila Thapar, I first learned that the Buddha was a historical person, and that early Buddhist texts in Pali revealed the society of his time in ways that other texts relating to Buddhism, as well as the Brahmanical literature, did not. In time I came to admire, more and more, the wisdom of the historical Buddha and so learned a lot about him over the years. It also seemed to me over this process of learning, and over the course of teaching the history of early South Asia, that the historical Buddha in my head did not really exist in the imagination of people, neither among Buddhists nor in others. I heard debates among Indian scholars who asked whether the Buddha was a historical person or an incarnation of Vishnu; my Chinese compatriots, both scholars and ordinarily serious readers, commonly mistook Amitabha or Maitreya for the Buddha; my students in America normally saw "the fat guy" who sat as a statue at the entrance of Chinese restaurants as the Buddha, a god who brought in wealth.

During the two decades I taught Indian and world histories at the College of New Jersey, I realised that even a lot of well-researched books, such as I.B. Horner's *Women under Primitive Buddhism* and Uma Chakravarti's *On the Social Philosophy of Buddhism*, barely provoked the imagination of students to try visualising the Buddha and his context and the lived life of his time. I understood that, in addition to the weighty scholarship, it was necessary, in order to approach a different kind of understanding, to look more closely at the Pali texts – albeit in English translation – including the *Jatakas*, the *Vinayas*, and so on. With these, my students seemed better able to engage in vigorous discussions about gender, religion, caste, and so on in early India. Their questions motivated me to write this book, in which I have attempted a reconstruction of the life of early Buddhist society. What I try to do here is show readers who some of the people were that we most frequently encounter in Buddhist narrations, what their contexts may have been like, and what the motives for and nature of their interactions were with Sakyamuni (the Buddha). So, I must thank all my students who inspired me to make real and material, in some sense, my admiration for the historical Buddha.

Compiling the scattered writings of a decade into a cohesive narrative during the Covid pandemic made me reflect on the similarities of the time of the Buddha and our current situation. There are of course large discrepancies in terms of the scale of the historical processes, but the personal agony and social traumas of the last two years have often made me feel I had seen all this in the time of the Buddha, and his reactions and responses and philosophical resolutions to the ailments of his day gave me hope. I hope equally that this book will reach, and perhaps teach, something of the Buddha's wisdom to those in India and abroad, and others in the Anglophone world who are interested in the historical cultures of Asia. I hope to publish a Chinese version of this book, to introduce those in China who remain interested in the historical Buddha, a little of what it was like to live in North India 2500 years ago.

With this broad audience centrally in mind, I have eliminated diacritical marks on proper names and special terms in my main narration. These marks have been retained in citations and references for readers who may want to pursue the sources. I have also adopted the spelling of Pali or Magadhi for proper names as recorded in the literature and inscriptions, these being closer to the language of the Buddha himself. Some of the terms used, such as Yakkho in Pali (Yaksha in Sanskrit), were in fact carved on stone statues of the named in Buddhist locations such as Bharhut. When the Mahayana Buddhist texts Sanskritised Buddhist terms, some of the early terms gained new meanings whereas others were not used or fell out of use. Sticking to the earlier spellings, I felt, would take us closer to the phonetic realms in which the Buddha spoke and help us hear some of the voices of that time, no matter how vaguely and tentatively.

Over the past decade I have relied on the scholarly strength of the University of Pennsylvania to carry out my research. Pushkar Sohoni, the South Asia librarian at the University of Pennsylvania, helped me access their precious photo archive funded by the American Institute of Indian Studies. Ramya Sreenivasan, chair of the Department of South Asian Regional Studies, invited me to present the chapter about women in their reputed South Asian seminar as long ago as 2013. Professor Deven Patel (of the same department) and I have discussed language issues over a cup tea on numerous occasions.

David Ludden, editor in chief of the online *Oxford Encyclopedia of Asian History*, invited me to write the entry on early Buddhism. To test the waters and get feedback, that entry was published online in April 2017: DOI: 10.1093 / acrefore / 9780190277727.013.22. After major revisions, this became the book's Introduction.

I was fortunate to participate in the symposium of the Romila Thapar *festschrift* in New Delhi, March 2019, and there present the first draft of the chapter here titled "Ahura and Asura: Persians and Indians in the Time of the Buddha". That essay was revised and published in *Questioning Paradigms, Constructing Histories*, ed. Kumkum Roy and Naina Dayal (New Delhi: Aleph, 2019). With helpful criticism from scholars and more research on the Persian side of the story, a revised version serves as Chapter 2 below.

Nearly forty years back Rukun Advani edited my first book, *Ancient India and Ancient China* (1988), which opened the door for my pursuit of an academic career. He has now edited this one. I know how utterly impossible it would have been for this book to have appeared in English without the comprehensive overhaul he has done of my non-native phrasings of English prose. I owe the publication of this book to him.

All is impossible without the support of my husband, Dr Weiye Li.

The book is dedicated, first of all, to my mentor Romila Thapar, who brought me into the world of early India. And to the late Professor Ludo Rocher and Professor Rosane Rocher, who taught me Sanskrit and Pali, providing me with the tools with which to explore that world.

Glossary

acchara/s	Magadhi name for *apsara*, a goddess associated with water
ahura/s	(In Persian usage) a Zoroastrian god; also designates Zoroastrians
apsara/s	Goddess associated with water
Aryavarta	Sacred land of the Aryas, the area between the Indus and Yamuna rivers
Atavi	Forest people
asura	(In Indian usage) an *ahura*; could also signify demi-god or creature lower than human
asava	Buddhist word for all kinds of addictive substances and addictions
Avesta	Zoroastrian sacred book
Balhika	Signifies Bactria in Buddhist literature
bhang / bhanga	Magadhi for cannabis
bhikkhu/s	Male member of Buddhist sangha
bhikkuni/s	Female member of Buddhist sangha
bodhisatta/s	Former incarnation of the Buddha
bhuta	Ghost; also designates a cult among mountainous communities
daha	Iranian for non-Aryans
dasa	Indian for people alien to the Vedic tradition

deva/s	Vedic god
devata/s	Heavenly beings; goddess in the heaven of *devas*
dhamma	Pali Buddhist word for *dharma*
gahapati	Householder; Pali for *grihapati*
Gandara	(In Persian usage) satrapy in the Indian north-west
Gandhara	(In Indian usage) Gandara
gandharva/s	Male heavenly musician and dancer
ganasangha	Polity comprising Ksatriya oligarchs
Hindush	Persian name for its satrapy in the Indus area
haoma / soma	Zoroastrian / Vedic terms for an intoxicating drink used in rituals
jataka/s	Story / stories of the Buddha's past lives
Khattiya	Pali for Ksatriya
Kosala	Pali for (the kingdom called) Koshala
Magadhi	Main language in the Greater Magadha region during the latter half of the first millennium BCE
mahajanapadas	"Great states" in Buddhist literature
naga/s	Snake; cobra; cobra cult; cobra-cult worshipper
Nagaraja	Chief of a cobra-cult community
nibbana	Pali for nirvana
niraya	Hell; antonym of nirvana
peta / peti	male / female ghosts; often restless beings connected with ancestors
Rajagaha	Magadhi name for Rajagriha, the capital of Magadha

rakshasa/s	Demon; alien creature in the wild
Sakka	Name for the god Indra in Buddhist texts
samana	Magadhi for *shramana* (*vide infra*)
sangha	organised body of Buddhists; assembly of disciples of the Buddha (or of the Jainas)
satrapy / satrap	Persian province / governor of Persian province
setthi	Pali for *shreshthi*, signifying the eldest or best within city elites
shramana	Followers of rival or other faiths
Taxila / Takshashila	Greek / Indian name for the political and cultural centre of Gandara / Gandhara
Ujjeni / Ujjayini	Magadhi / Sanskrit for Ujjain
Uposatha	Calendrical days for Buddhist *sangha* gatherings (usually two to four days each month)
Vajji Ganasangha	The most powerful *ganasangha* in the time of the Buddha
vanna	Pali for varna
Vesali	Pali for (the city of) Vaishali
vihara/s	Monastery; dwelling for Buddhist monks
Yakkha / Yakkhi	Pali for Yaksha / Yakshi (*vide infra*)
Yaksha / Yakshi	Male / female deities or sprites associated with nature and trees; also signfies community outside the Brahmanical mainstream
Yavanas / Yonas	Term for Greeks in India

1

The Time of the Buddha

Religions arose in many societies long before agriculture and pastoralism created the surpluses that led to urbanisation, and to the complex social structures by which large populations were sustained. Doctrines, as well as frequently performed rituals, probably helped shape a common identity within these large populations, leading to structured societies. Moralising religions emerged after the appearance of large and complex societies of more than a million people, with these often encompassing diverse ethnicities and several languages. The evocation of supernatural power within such moralising religions was intimidatory in intent, hanging over every head and threatening punishment to those who violated the morality and norms that, by consensus, were seen as necessary for social survival and development.[1]

Buddhism was one such moralising religion. It arose during a trying time, when state formation and urbanisation based on agricultural development had begun to take shape in South Asia. The Buddha, however, did not endorse a supreme god who exerted almighty and punitive power on those who violated the norms of morality; on the contrary, he created a cosmology in which the status of all living creatures could move up or down. Rewarding good behaviour and punishing bad deeds were believed to move creatures within a forever mobile hierarchy. This cosmology, which is the framework of the Buddhist religion – no matter the sect or school

---

[1] Whitehouse, *et al.*, "Complex Societies", pp. 227–9.

within it – has transformed the way of thinking about basic questions of life and death among its adherents and beyond. This success has been due in large part to the fact that the Buddha developed his doctrines from an understanding of the real and ground-level problems and sufferings within the society of his time.

Sakyamuni, meaning the wise man of the Sakya people, lived and spread his wisdom over a time of drastic change in South Asia. Cities, surrounded by farmlands, had begun to spring out of the fertile North Indian plains, primarily east of the confluence of the Yamuna and Ganges, in a region now referred to as Greater Magadha.[2] Meanwhile, trade had connected these cities to areas across the Hindu Kush Mountains in Central Asia; Achaemenid Persia had extended its territory all the way east to Kandahar in Afghanistan and Taxila on the upper Indus basin. Though geographically separated by the core region of Brahmanical culture – Aryavarta – the Persian and later the Greeks who occupied the north-west region of the subcontinent did communicate with Greater Magadha, where non-Brahmanical cultures and ideas flourished and rapid urbanisation was happening.

The Buddha's homeland, a small ganasangha – a Ksatriya clan oligarchy – was located in a stretch of the Himalayan foothills. This tiny state of the Sakyas had evolved commercially and politically alongside the rising kingdoms and ganasanghas of the middle and lower Ganges plain. From around the sixth century BCE – regarded as the time of the "second urbanisation" of South Asia – a variety of big and small new states in this region were constantly vying for hegemony and dominance through war and diplomacy. While the Sakyas co-ordinated irrigation for farming with neighbouring communities and suffered the inevitable skirmishes with them, their arch-enemy was the powerful Kosala kingdom which eventually, within the Buddha's lifetime, annihilated the Sakya ganasangha.

Siddhartha, a young man of the ganasangha, saw the cruelty of warfare and the socio-economic disparity that went hand in hand with increasing agricultural productivity and material abundance.

[2] This region is called "Greater Magadha" in Bronkhorst, *Greater Magadha*.

He was one of the earliest of those rare souls whose response focused most acutely on a specific aspect of social conditions, giving expression to it as the philosophical truth that the world is full of suffering and insecurity, and that the removal of these ills must be the goal of human endeavour. This observation evolved into the first and foremost truth within his doctrine of the Four Noble Truths.

It was a time when Brahmans and rajas, merchants and bankers, scribes and artisans, servants and slaves, courtesan-musicians and dancers, farmers and fishermen, and people from the mountains and forests all strove to move up, or at least maintain their status in the newly formed social hierarchy. Some of those from the low castes and outside the social core managed to get into the mainstream, but some never made it, and some born in elite families were cast out. The Buddhist sangha and other communities of dissidents were refuges for some of the unfortunate, while serving also as waystations for outsiders to get into the mainstream.

From stories embedded in early Buddhist texts, roughly contemporary Brahmana texts, and the earliest Buddhist artwork and messages inscribed on them, there hazily emerges the historical persona of the Buddha in the society of his time. Reconstructing the time of this historical Buddha means drawing mainly from the Pali canon, which is synonymous with the Buddhist texts preserved in Sri Lanka and the countries of South East Asia where Theravada Buddhist institutions kept such written documents. The Pali collection was the written-down form of the collective memory of the teachings of the Buddha. The first generation of disciples gathered after his passing to memorise what they had heard of his teachings. It took generations of Buddhist disciples to transform their memories into the written form of the Pali canon. Meanwhile, other early Buddhist texts survived in the Prakrit languages – for instance, in the Kharoshthi script of Gandharan Prakrit written on birch bark; of these, a number were dated to the first century CE. These manuscripts contain many texts known in the Pali Buddhist canon alongside some compositions comprising local stories unknown in the Pali collection.[3]

---

[3] Salomon, *Ancient Buddhist Scrolls from Gandhara*, pp. 7–11.

The Kharoshthi texts may conceivably have been written down earlier than the Pali canon, but the texts written on birch bark are fragments preserved in jars buried in monastic sites in the ancient Gandharan region. It is likely that both traditions drew from the same sources of the Greater Magadha region, but the sangha at Sri Lanka seems to have made the more faithful effort to stick to the Magadhi sources. Because the Theravada Buddhist tradition has been alive all the way down to modern times, the sangha there can be said to have preserved the earliest available texts pertaining to the Buddha. "Thera" were the elders of the sangha who memorised Buddhist teachings. Thus, Theravada was the school most persistent in preserving these earliest memories. The compiler of the Pali Buddhist canon, Buddhaghosha of the fifth century, claims that Magadhi was the same as Pali, the authentic language of the Buddha, and that therefore the Pali texts represent the most authentic canon of Buddhism.[4] No doubt there was also a transition from Magadhi to Pali which added vocabulary into these Pali texts, drawing from the development of Buddhism in South India. And moreover, since generations of Buddhist monk-scholars copied, edited, and commented on these manuscripts to preserve the original teachings of the Buddha, they inevitably revised and altered the original texts in spite of their best intention.

In 1888 a group of scholars led by T.W. Rhys Davids – who had served as a colonial civil servant in Ceylon and encountered remnants of Pali there – formed the Pali Text Society with the purpose of collecting, editing, and translating Buddhist Pali texts. Their readings of these reveal a Buddha and his time unknown in the Sanskrit, Chinese, and Tibetan Buddhist traditions. Their Buddha seems a much more real and historical character. Unlike the hagiographies that form part of the Sanskrit Buddhist texts, the Pali texts portray the Buddha and his major disciples as people striving to find solutions in a world full of painful dilemmas. These texts provide details of the processes by which the core Buddhist institution, the sangha, took shape step by step.

[4] Skilling, "Scriptural Authenticity", pp. 1–47 (11).

Since the time of the Pali Text Society's pioneering work in editing and translating several of these Pali texts, Indian historians – including D.D. Kosambi, J.P. Sharma, Romilar Thapar, and Uma Chakravarti – have striven to reconstruct the political, social, and economic conditions of the Buddha's time by drawing information, albeit critically, from the Pali Buddhist texts, the only literature that could have survived from around the time of the Buddha or very likely soon after. In her book on the historiography of early India, *The Past Before Us* (2013), Romila Thapar affirms the historical value of Pali Buddhist texts when saying that "the Buddha was a historical person whose life was seen by Buddhists not only as ethically exemplary but also a turning point in history."[5] Among the Pali texts is the *Vinaya Pitaka*, containing the disciplinary rules of the Buddhist sangha, which makes it especially valuable as a source of information for historians since it "describes the formation of the Buddhist community. Events are given a chronology."[6] This chronology is associated with the rulers of the time and from it emerges a sketchy picture of the political situation. Collectively, the Pali texts provide stories of monks, nuns, rich and poor patrons, and the Buddha's followers from the peripheries of his society. A group of Pali texts in a category called *Khuddaka-nikaya* (or Minor Texts) – including *Vimanavatthu, Peta-Vatthu, Jataka,* and *Apadana* – also provide much information, though they probably took shape much after the major texts. They comprise, in the main, didactic stories that could well have served as manuals for preaching and teaching.[7] The vagaries and uncertainties of circulation in the ancient world no doubt enhanced the value of some of these texts while diminishing the value of others, but the basic fact remains that their story lines fall within the geo-social context of Greater Magadha over the time of the Buddha. Thus it is reasonable to assume that the stories handed down in these texts contain something like a common memory of the time and society of the Buddha.

[5] Thapar, *The Past Before Us*, p. 381.
[6] Ibid., p. 399.
[7] Skilling, "Scriptural Authenticity", pp. 31, 36.

Archaeological digs during the nineteenth and twentieth centuries discovered the edicts of Ashoka, the third king of the Mauryan Empire, who reigned in the third century BCE, as well as Buddhist monuments dated to Ashoka's time and later. Epigraphic and palaeo-philological researches on inscriptions in the Greater Magadha region have demonstrated the similarity of language, syntax, and vocabulary between the inscriptions and the Pali texts. Artwork on several Buddhist monuments which appeared after Ashoka and the Mauryans depicts many of the characters and stories described in the Pali texts, especially those in the *Digha Nikaya* – a memorised record of the earliest teachings of the Buddha. These sculptural scenes on stupas in the Greater Magadha region were visual memories of the time of the Buddha. The Buddhist community in Sri Lanka, the major base for the preservation of the Pali textual tradition, has over the centuries regularly made pilgrimages and donations to Bodh Gaya, where the Buddha found enlightenment. Buddhist scholarship in Sri Lanka has therefore been closely connected to the earliest Buddhist site to maintain the authenticity of the Buddha's teachings as preserved by the community.

Stupas constructed since the time of Ashoka fanned out from the home region of the Buddha – the middle and lower Ganges plain – down to the Deccan Plateau. The narratives in their artwork all carry the imprints of the original locations of the stories they tell – Vesali (Vaishali), Savatthi (Sravasti), Rajagaha (Rajagriha). The sacred geography created by the early stupas has consequently resulted in a Buddhist identity among communities within and outside the domain of the Sanskrit and Prakrit languages.[8] Pali texts, inscriptions, and the artwork on Buddhist monuments have recorded the memories that made possible a historical narrative of the life of the Buddha and his time.

South Asia from the Buddha to Ashoka

The world of the Buddha in the Ganges plain was one in which the rajas of kingdoms and ganasanghas ruled over an elite class, as well

---

[8] Ray, "The Archaeology of Stupas", pp. 3–19.

as a new urban upper class comprising gahapatis (householders) and setthis (elders and financiers). Collectively, this class dominated everyday life. The daily life of the new urban households had, however, to be supported by the new class of workers who maintained basic sanitation in the cities. The Candalas were people outside the caste hierarchy – they were the outcast. They cleaned out the garbage and trash from streets; inevitably they looked dirty and smelt bad and so were considered polluting, even though they were indispensable for making the city liveable. As they were pushed out of sight, their communication with the urban residents they served was minimal. The Candalas may well have evolved their own dialect within their own community, either based on the language they spoke before they joined urban life, or perhaps a pidgin variety of the language used by the people they served.

The political and economic networks of the ruling class also absorbed communities that lived on the peripheries of this society. Such communities included people who were out of the cultural pale of the Sanskrit- and Prakrit-speaking agricultural and urban zones. The Buddhist sangha flourished in the interface areas, with the sangha's monks and nuns wandering through the agricultural urban core as well as over mountains and marshlands where could be found a variety of cults – of Naga (cobra), Yakkhas (Yakshas), and kinnaras (half-human, half-animal creatures). The sangha's effort seems by contrast to have been to establish a simple and healthy lifestyle in relation to diet, clothing, hygiene, and sanitation, and this simplicity began to attract admiration and support among peoples of the various surrounding cultures.

From his observation of the nature and culture of his surroundings, the Buddha seems to have created a visionary universe encompassing all living creatures into a hierarchy notable for its flexibility. By positing a scheme in which the nature of rebirth depended on the quality of deeds done within a lifespan, it became possible for any living creature to move up the scale in its next life on account of having acquired merit through virtuous deeds performed in this life. Even the lowest ghost in hell could move up towards the domain of animals, asuras (aliens, especially Persians), humans, and the heaven of the Brahmanical god Indra, even if the ascent to godhead could take many lifespans. Meanwhile, bad behaviour could overcome merit and push the creature down to a lower level. This universe made room for hope and inspiration for everyone, including the despised poor and the feared savage, to aspire to a future life of dignity and respect.

Buddhist cosmology evolved in the geo-political and socio-economic environment of its time. The small Ksatriya oligarchy located on the fringes of the urban core of the Ganges plain from which the Buddha emerged was the storm centre of rising monarchies such as Kosala and Magadha, and ganasanghas that included the Vajji Confederacy – a grouping of several contiguous clans. In these many ganasanghas the Ksatriya elites made collective decisions on major state affairs and jealously guarded their blood purity, which meant ensuring their caste superiority by banning marriages with clans outside their own lineages. The Sakyas, for instance, traced their ancestry to a Ksatriya clan banished to the Himalaya foothills where the men had married their sisters to keep their lineage pure.[9] The Licchavis, a ganasangha in the Vajji Confederacy, tried purifying their Ksatriya status by staging an annual bathing ceremony in a sacred pond within their capital city, Vesali.[10]

The powerful kingdoms, such as Kosala and Magadha, allied with others, and meanwhile conquered some of the smaller kingdoms and ganasanghas. Eventually, Magadha annexed the Vajji Ganasangha Confederacy and had built the Mauryan Empire by the late fourth century BCE. A time of conquest and annexation might in itself have suggested the wisdom – or its extension and exalted form "enlightenment" – in actively engaging communities on all sides in order to mediate bloody conflict and reduce everyday suffering among the population at large.

While the Buddha and his sangha traversed the cities on the Ganges, the exchange of commodities and ideas linked the new

---

[9] Rhys Davids, trans. *Dialogues of the Buddha*, D.i.III.16, pp. 114–15.

[10] The sacred pond of Vesali had been maintained for many centuries, as witnessed by Chinese pilgrims. Archaeological excavation has restored this pond. See Falk, *Asokan Sites and Artefacts*, p. 220.

urban core with the north-west section of the subcontinent. On the upper Indus valley Taxila became an international metropolis. It had all started with the eastward expansion of the Achaemenid Persian Empire. In present-day Afghanistan and the Punjab region of Pakistan, the Persian Empire had by the end of the sixth century BCE set up three satrapies – Bactria, Gandara (Gandhara), and Hindush. The satraps here were military governors assigned to these regions by Persian kings. Their major tasks were maintaining local order and sending tribute to the capitals at Susa and Persepolis. Persian governance of these routes also facilitated migrations between the various regions of a vast Persian empire stretching from Ionia to the north-west corner of South Asia.

After crushing the Persian army of Darius III, Alexander of Macedonia had marched into the Indus Valley around 326 BCE. Soon after, he had retreated from India leaving soldiers in garrison towns named Alexandria, including those at what are now Kandahar and Ai-Khanoum on the Oxus. After Alexander's death in 323 BCE his general, Seleucus Nikator, carved out the Seleucid Empire, which went from Mesopotamia to Central Asia and neighboured the rising Mauryan Empire. After Ashoka ascended the throne (c. 268 BCE), parts of Afghanistan and Punjab were integrated into the Mauryan Empire. The territory controlled by Ashoka thus included the cosmopolitan area centred at Taxila, where there was a Hellenistic neighbourhood adjacent to the former Persian governor's headquarters. Under the powerful Mauryan Empire the Greater Magadha region continued to defy Brahmanisation, primarily on account of the dynasty's own rise from a region in which many non-Brahmanical traditions flourished.

Sakyamuni and the Sakya People

The Buddha never saw his mother, who seems not to have long survived his birth. The earliest of his life experiences made him dwell on the "suffering of birth and death". Pajapati Gotami, his aunt, breast-fed him and raised him; she is believed to have loved her foster son and helped bring his message to the Sakya people. She was a woman allowed into the sangha at a time when no woman had been so permitted. When Sakyamuni preached in Kapilavastu, his home town, this aunt Pajapati saw it as an opportunity to plead for women being allowed to join the sangha.[11] After two more failed attempts – probably because the Sakya ganasangha was conquered by the Kosala king Vidudabha – Pajapati led Sakya women and walked all the way to Vesali, where the Buddha had taken up his abode, to join the sangha. There she cut off her hair, donned orange-coloured robes as bhikkhus (mendicants) did; her feet were swollen and her clothes dusty after the long journey, and she wept tears while waiting outside the preaching hall for the Buddha to answer her plea to join the sangha. Seeing her miserable condition, Ananda, the Buddha's most loyal disciple, who was also a Sakya, went into the preaching hall to exhort, on behalf of the women, that they be allowed to join the sangha. The Buddha was unmoved yet again. Ananda then changed his approach by asking whether women, in the teaching of the Buddha himself, could reach enlightenment. When his master confirmed that women were indeed capable of enlightenment, Ananda pushed his argument further.[12] At which point the Buddha nodded his head, granting permission to women to join the sangha. Pajapati thereafter came to be known as Maha Pajapati (the Great Pajapati), superintendent of the bhikkhunis (nuns) of the sangha.

The Buddha's Supporters in Cities

The cities of North India in this period were similar to Athens and other ancient Greek cities in that not all people living within them had equal political rights. In the ganasanghas, women had no say in public affairs. Only adult men who were the heads of their households had full rights to participate in public affairs. Such men were also called "raja", their title within their households being that of the king. In a small ganasangha such as that of the Sakyas, there were

---

[11] Rhys Davids, trans., *Vinaya Texts*, Cullavagga, x, 1, pp. 320–7. The following story is from this passage.

[12] Ibid., p. 322.

about 500 such household rajas. In the city of Vesali, a common saying was that 7707 Licchavi rajas lived in the city. Though these numbers were proverbial rather than real, they do indicate extraordinary differences in the sizes of cities at the time.

In fact, the total population of a city was far larger than suggested by the number of fully empowered household rajas. Women, children, and young adult males awaiting their turn to become rajas of a Licchavi lineage were also resident in these cities, and moreover not all those resident in Vesali belonged to a Licchavi lineage. Cities were places of opportunity, so that many from a variety of different backgrounds moved into them, looking for ways to improve their lot in life. Though these outsiders could not join the Licchavis in voting during the making of public decisions, they could find jobs or set themselves up in businesses involving crafts and some form of trade. Perhaps most importantly, people of disadvantaged family backgrounds could leave their birth status behind in their villages or pastoral tribes to assume a new social status based on new-found pursuits in the cities.

Urban life, a new social and economic phenomenon in North India, thus attracted many to cities such as Vesali. These were bustling urban areas replete with new people, new ideas, and new professions. Altered lives also meant alternative outlooks, attitudes, and worldviews which challenged prescriptive Brahmanical norms embodied in the caste system. City immigrants had in essence escaped their original caste affiliations and could hide low-birth origins by denying association with the caste system. In the cities the labour of these newcomers was in high demand: urban life always requires skilled professionals such as scribes and physicians, and poorly paid labourers who keep cities clean and do the work that the well-off look down on.

The breaching of caste walls was not limited to these city newcomers. In Magadha military men who gained power called themselves rajas, and no one was going to set about making inquiries about their birth status. The Licchavis, the ruling elite of Vesali and of the Vajji Confederacy, however, said their own origins lay in the

Solar Lineage, one of the two most prestigious Ksatriya lineages. While the Licchavis lived in Vesali and managed their public affairs collectively through discussion, debate, ritual ceremony, and the election of a chief raja as well as administrators, the Magadha monarchy ruled from Rajagaha, being assisted by Brahman priests and affluent householders and financiers. The Magadha kingdom claimed the most fertile rice paddy lands, the iron ore mines, and forests where elephants roamed. Traders and professionals travelled from city to city even as the rajas in Vesali and the raja in Rajagaha watched every political move made by their rivals.

In the confrontation between the most powerful monarchy and the largest ganasangha, the Buddha clearly took the side of Vesali. When staying in that city, he taught the Vajjians a strategy that could win the war against Magadha. This was that they must meet regularly, as ordained by their tradition, and act in concord; that they should respect the ancient Vajjian institutions; that they should defer to elders and listen to their advice; that they must not violate women against their will; that they ought to make oblations and maintain their old shrines; and that they should protect and offer alms to religious recluses.[13] In other words, he was saying: You Vajjians already have all the institutions you need to keep yourselves strong in the defence of your way of life. You must maintain solidarity and follow your valuable traditions if you are to avoid defeat by your most powerful enemy.

When the Buddha stayed in Vulture's Peak near Rajagaha, the capital of Magadha, its king Ajatasattu (Ajatashatru) sent his minister, a Brahman named Vassakara, to solicit the sage's advice. The Buddha told the shrewd Brahman that the Vajjians could not be defeated because they were following all their hallowed traditions, these being the very principles the Buddha had preached to his sangha.[14]

On account of his respect for the ganasangha traditions of the Licchavis and the Vajji Confederacy, the Buddha made several trips

---

[13] *Dialogues of the Buddha*, D.ii.74–5, pp. 80–1.
[14] Ibid., 76–7, pp. 81–3.

to Vesali to provide moral support and guidance. When in Vesali, the chief courtesan of the city, Ambapali, was his hostess, offering him and his followers a big vegetarian feast. Though Ambapali was a courtesan, the Buddha, over his stay in the Ambapali Garden and his feast at her house, never saw her as a prostitute. Despite the proliferation of supposedly "fallen women" – they were mainly entertainers and performers of dance and music in the newly developed urban centres – the Buddha's view of Ambapali seems to have been uncommonly sane: he treated her as a representative of the Licchavis and the city of Vesali.

However, despite the advice the Buddha gave them, the Vajjians lost their battle against Magadha. Vassakara, the Brahman minister of Magadha, apparently sent spies to Vesali to spread rumours and provoke disputes and was successful in fomenting internecine war. The Vajjians fought amongst themselves and lost the force of will with which they had long defended themselves against external enemies.

Forests, Mountains, and Waters

Around the cities were cultivated fields and pastures dotted by villages where most residents were peasant farmers, largely Sudras and outcastes. Though low-status people, they belonged all the same within the Brahmanical cultural domain, sharing their understanding of languages and religious concepts with urban folk. Further from the cities, along routes linking them, lived people who were either exiles from mainstream society or original inhabitants of the mountains, forests, and marshlands. Because such populations did not share the languages and values of the new state culture, they and their norms were seen as irrelevant or beyond the pale by city and village people. However, they did have contact and interaction with the saints and ascetics of various religious sects who chose to leave the noise of the cities to dwell in worlds of thought and practise their religion in the more sylvan environment of forests. Conversely, many hunters and fishermen, having heard of the fantastic lives it was possible to lead in cities, sought opportunities there. Such men and women settled into various jobs and professions, high or low, whatever they managed to find. They were looked down on by the urban and regarded with suspicion. Meanwhile the communities they came from – people who worshipped snakes, trees, tree spirits – were not located all that far from the outskirts of cities. Among them were those who had not ventured for work into the cities, who had preferred staying where they were, sometimes to rob those traversing the countryside to ply their trade. There were always unwary or isolated travellers on routes that cut through forests, mountains, and rough terrain, all liable to be relieved of their goods by wayside bandits.

The dominant cultural domain may have been within the upper strata of states built by Indo-European-speaking communities spread across the Indus and Gangetic plains, but the people of the forests and marshlands, even if less powerful and disorganised, carried some weight within the economy. They not only populated the cities with fresh blood, they also provided cities and villages with the products of forests and mountains and waters, including iron ore and minerals, trained elephants for labour, meat from jungles, and fish from waterbodies. With the expansion of agriculture, the territories of these wild people tended to retreat more and more into the deep mountains and forests, though without ever totally disappearing.

Around 1000 BCE, the Vedic people had migrated eastwards along the plains that lay between the foothills of the Himalaya and the river Ganges. To wrest or claim lands that belonged to the indigenous population, they had had to pacify the local inhabitants through coercion and diplomacy. This meant, first, having to learn how to deal with the deities worshipped by local communities. When Brahman priests administered the horse sacrifice in Vedic societies, the rituals lasted an entire year in order to help a chief lay effective claim to the territory under his control. In these ceremonies we see priests trying to position and accommodate diverse cults, Vedic and non-Vedic, into a reshaped Vedic universe. Both devas and asuras originated when Indo-European speakers split into an Iranian branch and an Indian branch around Afghanistan. While ahuras became the dominant gods in the cosmology of Iranian culture, asuras became the arch-enemies of the devas in the Indian Vedic literature. Within the horse sacrifice, Brahman priests reserved certain days for the worship of various spirits, ranging from ancestors to ghosts, to convey the contours of their universe. On the seventh day of the ceremony, they allowed the asuras to stay and practice their magic.[15] That asuras frequently appear in late-Vedic literature and early-Buddhist Pali texts indicates that asuras, as the adversary of the devas, remained in the Indian cosmos. The Iranian branch of Indo-European speakers, who were mostly settled in West Asia and worshipped ahuras, were probably identified as asuras by those already resident in India when the ahura worshippers migrated into India, settling there and mingling with the local population.

With cities appearing on the Ganges plain and the Iranian Achaemenid Empire having extended its territory to the north-western area of the subcontinent with its administrative centre at Taxila, Aramaic – the lingua franca of the Persian Empire – prevailed in the north-west area for several centuries. It is reasonable to assume that people of Iranian culture who worshipped ahuras lived around the city of Taxila, and probably also in the cities of the Ganges plain, where they were called asuras by their Indian hosts.

In the horse sacrifice ceremonies Brahman priests also addressed lesser spirits, such as female celestial beings called apsaras and male ones called gandharvas, these being musicians and dancers.[16] There were also some less beautiful beings they needed to deal with, such as the king of the snakes, who headed the many snake cults spread across India; and King Kubera Vaisravana, a god who commanded many nasty beings such as rakshasas, villains, and robbers (*papakrita, selaga*).[17] Though these various spirits received different levels of respect in the ceremonies, none were totally banished from

---

[15] Eggeling, trans., *Satapatha Brahmana*, XIII.4.3.11, p. 368.
[16] Ibid., 4.4.7–8, pp. 365–6.
[17] Ibid., 4.4.9–10, pp. 367–8.

Brahmanical sacred space. Kubera became a popular deity within many religious sects and was known as the commander of the Yakkhas (Yakshas in Sanskrit), these Yakkhas being a variety of creatures in human form, male and female. Some of them were benign and beautiful, others bloodthirsty and ugly, the whole an ensemble of robbers and thugs under the command of Kubera. In short, late-Vedic rituals included while also marginalising the cults of indigenous communities.

During the middle of the first millennium BCE, when states formed in most of the North Indian plain, the Buddha and other thinkers of his ilk were face to face with this colourful cosmos of deities, ranging from those of the Vedic traditions to those of the various cults worshipped by people migrating into villages and cities or who lived in forests and marshlands. Cults of Yakkhas, Nagas, apsaras, and gandharvas permeated all corners of this world and every new school of faith. Religious schools recruited their members from the communities who belonged to these cults, and people seem to have generally adhered to their cults even after joining the new faith. Theologians of the Jainas, Brahmans, and Buddhists all tried to conceptualise the plethora of spirits into some kind of system, and thus ended up with varying hierarchies depending on their own perspective of the universe.[18] Early Buddhists abhorred alcohol and blood sacrifices in Yakkha, Naga, and rituals of other such cults, but they did not condemn the cults as offensive.[19]

The Sangha of the Buddha and His Society

To approximate an understanding of society in the Buddha's time, recourse to definitive sources dating to about three hundred years later, when Ashoka consolidated the Mauryan Empire in the third century BCE, is pretty much inevitable. Ashoka held sway over much of the subcontinent, and in his time the contrast between state societies and "outsiders" became much clearer. In his famous Thirteenth

---

[18] Decaroli, *Haunting the Buddha*, pp. 10ff.
[19] Ibid., pp. 24–5.

Edict, which inscribes his psychological devastation and moral regeneration in the aftermath of the Kalinga war and enunciates his determination of peaceful governance, Ashoka categorises his subjects as "Brahmana, Sramana, and all sects [*prashamda* or *pasamda*], and householders". Whatever their faiths, and whether they were religious figures or secular followers, these were now within the empire's mainstream and had to abide by his dhamma – the law and moral rules. Even the Greeks, called Yona by Ashoka, fell within the fold of the law-abiding subjects of his empire, though their religion was quite different from the one established by the emperor. Those who lived in forests, the Atavi – people who were not members of any of the recognisable religions but belonged to fancy cults of snakes, half-humans, and "ugly" humans – were given Ashoka's word that his policy of peace extended to them so long as they made no trouble in the settlements of his own people; if not, they needed to beware harsh punishment.[20]

Ashoka's empire reached the apex of the second urbanisation of the subcontinent with the addition of the solid infrastructure of a Northern Royal Highway and a Southern Royal Highway. These royal highways were lined with trees and resting houses and garrisoned by a standing army. These were the roads that connected urban dwellers with communities of different cultures and languages in the peripheries, people who sometimes came out and at other times retreated to their forested or wetland terrains.

The roads were not the only threads linking diverse peoples. Over the three hundred years or so of state development separating the Buddha and Ashoka, the former's sangha, Brahman rishis, the Jaina sangha, and other dissident religious communities forged another link between settled and urbanising civilisation with the peripatetic, the itinerant, and those in the hinterland. There is clear evidence of the dwellings of religious communities in deep forests, of missionary activities introducing cults and people there to the settled

---

[20] The two passages appear in several versions of the XIII Major Rock Inscriptions of Ashoka: Hultzsch, trans., *Inscriptions of Asoka*, vol. I.

world. In much of the early religious literature, women from obscure backgrounds feature as consorts or as the mothers of major heroes in legends about state-creation. Shakuntala, the mother of Bharata – the greatest ancestral king in the Brahmanical tradition – was an apsara, or the daughter of an apsara, a beautiful woman with no traceable family. Her story first appears in the *Satapatha Brahmana*, which is part of the later Vedic literature focused on Vedic migration settlements in the Ganges plain.[21] The legend of Shakuntala then flourishes in the Mahabharata and other classical Sanskrit literature. In Buddhist Pali literature, a jataka story relates a similar plot, though without the name Shakuntala. The setting is the usual jataka story of a time when King Brahmadatta ruled Benares. The king wanders into the woods, where he encounters a girl gathering faggots. The king gives a signet ring to the girl as a token of remembrance if a boy happens to be born from their encounter. However, the king denies their union when his son arrives at court along with his mother, despite being shown the signet ring as evidence. The boy in this version is the Buddha in a former birth, i.e. a bodhisatta. The woman, whose name we never learn, challenges the king by throwing the boy into the air, swearing that no true prince ever falls to the ground; miraculously, the boy lands on the lap of the king. In due course he inherits the throne with the title King Kattavahan, meaning "faggot bearer".[22] Shakuntala, the faggot-gathering girl, represents women of obscure background from the peripheries who gain status by fighting for the inheritance and other rights of their sons. Most women from these marginal lands never acquired Shakuntala's fame or status, but several were assimilated into the mainstream because of the interface created by religious vanguards who made their way into the peripheries. Regarding the various religious traditions that Ashoka later recognised as legitimate schools of thought and faith, an abundant Buddhist literature and artwork on monuments allow us some insight into the origins and activities of women generically denoted by Shakuntala.

[21] Romila Thapar analyses the Shakuntala legend from antiquity to modern times in idem, *Sakuntala*, pp. 10–11.
[22] Chalmers, trans., *Jatakas* no. 7, *Jataka Stories*, vol. I, pp. 27–9.

The Sakya people, alongside the Magadhas, Kosalas, and Vajjis, etc., all spoke a vernacular derivative of Sanskrit. The dialects may have varied but they all had Indo-European roots. In their speech they differed from speakers of both Vedic Sanskrit as well as the early classical Sanskrit defined by the Brahmanical grammarian Panini. In other words, the Middle and Lower Ganges catchment was the frontier of orthodox Brahmanical culture at the edge of Aryavarta – the supposedly pure land of Aryans.[23] The Pali language, which provides records of the earliest Buddhist speech, was probably a canonical concordance of the dialects of the region. The ruling elite and lettered people here did not speak Sanskrit but nevertheless considered themselves "Arya" (Aya in Pali), much as did Brahmans living in the so-called Aryavarta.

The urban centres of the region, as already noted, were well connected with each other and the world beyond – namely the more developed habitations of West Asia via the city of Taxila in the Indus valley, and the less developed mountainous areas to the south from where the Magadhans obtained elephants, timber, and iron ore. To acquisition such resources, enterprising setthis and gahapatis (traders) had to deal with people outside their own cultural framework, i.e. with those who spoke a different language and worshipped their own gods. Such communities, which lay outside the cultural domain of the Indo-European speakers, seem to have often assimilated into the dominant society through marriage alliances and associated rituals. These several subordinate communities who assimilated with the mainstream were not always male-dominant patriarchal lineages. Many of the Buddha's disciples came from communities in which mother figures had a higher status than the *pater familius*. Sariputta, meaning "son of Sari", was one of the Buddha's reputed disciples whose name was an extension of his mother's. A close bond between mothers and sons was a common phenomenon among the adherents of early Buddhism. Instead of male ancestor worship, these Buddhists concerned themselves more with the well-being of

---

[23] The heterodox features of the regions are well discussed in the Introduction by Bronkhorst, *Greater Magadha*, pp. 1–9.

deceased mothers. The universe of Sakyamuni, filled with a host of spirits, was one in which the dominant deities were male, but the more numerous deities were female. Those in the Vedic pantheon – as in the cults that joined hands within Vedic clan assemblies and are spoken of in the *Satapatha Brahmana* – were mostly male. The supreme Vedic hero, Indra, was still the dominant figure overseeing the universe at the time of the Buddha. Under the name of Sakka he interferes, mostly positively, within incidents narrated about the former lives of the Buddha. His heaven of thirty-three devas translates into a heaven of women who cook and serve in the Buddhist sangha but do not manage to join the sangha during their lifetime. In this heaven the devatas are virtuous ladies who reside in heavenly mansions and command huge retinues of female musicians and dancers, the accharas – the Pali version of apsaras. The achievements of these devatas are argued as exemplary, being used as educational materials to persuade Buddhist women to support the sangha by feeding bhikkhus and bhikkhunis. Those providing food to members of the sangha on a daily basis acquired enough merit to be elevated to this heaven. Moggallana, the great disciple of the Buddha whose origins lay in a matrilineal community, constantly brings such a message down from Sakka's heaven to the world, this being expounded in a Buddhist Pali text, *Vimanavatthu* (Stories of Mansions).

Though operating a patriarchal system of power and property inheritance, the new states and cities were also clearly recruiting members from matrilineal communities that were engaged in hunting, fishing, and gathering. From the margins, in other words – from forests, mountains, and waters outside the region of villages surrounded by rice paddy lands – came many outstanding women who became leaders of the new states in their urban centres, such as Ambapali of Vesali and the legendary Shakuntala. Only a few women, however, entered the inner circles of power in these newly founded states. Most women who found their way to the cities from the margins filled other urban roles. Salavati, a courtesan in Rajagaha, established a business around entertainment and prostitution in the city. Jivaka, a physician, and Sirima, a courtesan, both born of Salavati, followed different paths when they integrated into urban society. Jivaka went all the way to Taxila to study medicine, then returned to Rajagaha as a great physician. Sirima inherited her mother's profession as head entertainer in the Magadhan capital. Both were strong supporters of the Buddhist sangha because there was no place for them in the orthodox Brahmanical hierarchy, whereas they could with their services and donations fit comfortably into the social networks of Buddhist lay followers.

More such women have their donations recorded on the Sanchi and Bharhut stupas, and in their own names; and the names show their association with the Naga, Yakkha (or Yakkhi), or Bhuta communities. These possibly matrilineal communities were certainly silent followers of the Buddha. They may have spoken languages incomprehensible to the more settled population, but the Buddha seems to have had a special rapport with such folk. Their support could have been encouragement to their sons to join the sangha. Sariputta was the son of Rupasari, and Moggallana was the son of Moggali.[24] Bhikkhus and bhikkhunis from matrilineal communities, or born of women who had no legitimate husbands, served as bridges between on the one hand mainstream society following various religious schools – termed sramana and pasanda by Ashoka – and on the other the Atavi, people who, in the same terminology, lived in and roamed the forests and who could turn out to be harmful intruders.

According to the doctrines of Buddhism, the sons and daughters of women who joined the sangha were expected to sever all attachment to their families, regardless of their social status. The purpose of becoming a follower of the Buddha was, after all, to liberate oneself from the cycles of rebirth. Ancestor worship – the core religious ritual in a patriarchal regime – was not a legitimate pursuit for a bhikkhu. The *Peta-Vatthu*, one of the Minor Texts, addressed the tension

---

[24] Rhys Davids, trans., *Therāgatha*, CCLIX, *Sariputta* commentary, *Psalms of the Early Buddhists, II; Psalms of the Brethren*, pp. 340–1.

between the faithfulness of a bhikkhu and piety to ancestors. The word for ancestor, peta (father), denoted a kind of pitiful ghost wandering the universe, unable to settle. Ghosts were in this condition because they had not earned merit enough to be reborn with an improved status. Stories in the *Peta-Vatthu* told Buddhist followers that ancestors who had fallen into this misery of ghosthood retained the possibility of salvation through the meritorious acts of their progeny and descendants. The attachment among Buddhist disciples to deceased mothers lingering in these narratives is evidence of belief in the rebirth scheme. In one of these stories, Sariputta together with Moggallana and some others once stayed in a forest not far from Rajagaha. A woman who had been the mother of Sariputta several births earlier had been reborn as an ugly flesh-eating ghost, a peti (female ancestor) doomed to wander in the forest because she had served vile food to bhikkhus, and cursed them for good measure. Having been his mother once, she appealed to Sariputta for help. He took pity on her. Along with Moggallana and three other brothers they all trooped off to the court of King Bimbisara to solicit four cabins in the forest as his gift to the sangha. When the cabins, well fitted and with a water supply, had been built, Sariputta assigned the credit accruing from this noble deed to his former mother. She was thus able to shake off her sad peti condition, reach a deva birth, and progress into becoming a devata.[25] This intriguing story, attributed to Sariputta, was probably composed a century or two after his entire generation of elders in the sangha had passed away. With the Buddhist sangha expanding deeper into forest regions, where matrilineal communities were to be found, ties to female ancestors had somehow to be made manifest in Buddhist stories for the hegemonic purposes of extending Buddhist doctrine into the lives of culturally different and therefore possibly sceptical audiences.

Women from the margins, during and after Ashoka's empire, show a strong presence in the earliest Buddhist art. Sculptural art

---

[25] Gehman, trans., *Peta-Vatthu*, Book II, *Stories of the Departed*, pp. 29–30.

flourished in the Mauryan Empire, especially during the reign of Ashoka, whose pillar edicts are exquisite monuments of an empire and its ideals. The stupas at Sanchi in Central India were also likely built in his time, probably with his patronage, this being testified by a pillar carved with one of his edicts standing just beside the major stupa.

From the arrangement of the stupa and the pillar edict, it seems plausible to infer that Ashoka had the Buddhist monument built here because he trusted the sangha as comprising missionaries pacifying the Naga tribes of the forest. The Buddha had not designated a successor for the sangha when he passed away, but the sangha soon established institutional regulations to study his teachings and discipline the lives of Buddhist monks and nuns. They gathered, for instance, on the days of Uposatha – the day preceding the four stages of the waxing and waning of the moon – and twice a month if there was a major agenda. More events could be added for urgent needs in between the two, but no more than four within the term of a single moon.

Though the charismatic teacher had departed, stupas with his relics symbolised his continuing presence among them. Ashoka had several stupas built to provide facilities for sangha gatherings, the Sanchi Stupa being one such. The Sanchi monastic complex lay deep in a Deccan forest, along one of the routes connecting Kosambi in the Ganges plain to the ports of the western coastal region. The stupa was constructed as a bare dome containing the relics of the Buddha, but no image of the Buddha. After Ashoka, Sanchi developed into a monastery and two more stupas were added. There were now numerous sculptures of a variety of cults – awesome Nagas, beautiful Yakkhis, ghost-like human figures, and many kinds of kinnaras on the stone railings surrounding the stupa. The sculptures and reliefs were executed with donations from both those who visited from Vedisa (Vidisha) city – capital of the Sunga Dynasty which succeeded the Mauryan Empire in the Great Magadha region – and those outside the boundaries of settled people. These donors identified themselves by the names of Nagas, Yakkhas, and Bhutas. As mentioned above, a number of them with names linked to such tribes were women. Relief panels on the southern gate's arch of Stupa 1, the main entrance accessing the dome, depict scenes of Ashoka's patronage and jataka stories. On the middle crossbar of the arch, the most suitable position for a visual message, a scene shows Ashoka riding a royal chariot and approaching a stupa from the left side, followed by a large retinue of horse riders, elephant riders, and pedestrians, with winged creatures hovering above. On the other side of the central stupa, a Naga king wearing a hood of five cobra heads approaches the same stupa surrounded by a retinue of men and women wearing hoods of one or more cobra heads. The Naga king is also protected by winged kinnaras in the same majestic manner. Several smaller panels on the pillar of the arch depict Ashoka's visits to the Bodhi tree and to stupas in a less ornate style. A relief which shows Ashoka grieving while worshipping a lock of the Buddha's hair is signed by a guild of ivory carvers from the city of Vedisa.[26] The Sunga Dynasty, which claimed Brahman lineage, had built their new capital at a distance from the Mauryan capital Pataliputra. But the memory of Ashoka, despite being in what was earlier a frontier region and now the metropolis of the new regime, persisted. This is clear from several signed works by ivory artisans and donors from Vedisa and localities in the environs of Sanchi.

All these artworks were made after Ashoka's time, when the Mauryans no longer controlled the region. In Ashoka's day, when the stupa was built, Sanchi was one of the frontier posts of the state establishment. The king seems to have liked seeing properly dressed and well-behaved Buddhist bhikkhus and bhikkhunis engaged in conveying the Buddha's teachings to forest dwellers. The communities of Nagas and Yakkhas and Nishadas and so on were naked savages in need of pacifying and the salvific ideas embodied in dhamma. It is evident that when the major panel of Sanchi's south gate was executed, showing both Ashoka and a Naga king worshipping the stupa, the Mauryan regime was no longer in power, having

---

[26] Ibid., vol. I, 342, no. 400; American Institute of Indian Studies, neg. no. 320.95.

been replaced by a regime of cobra worshippers under the Sunga regime.[27] Though Ashoka's sons and grandsons were no longer rulers, the emperor's interest in converting forest people to Buddhism seems to have borne fruit, to the extent that his memory in supporting the mission was honoured in sculpted artwork.

---

[27] Joseph Schwartzberg marks the territory of the Nagas in this region (EF4 of Plate 21a): idem, *A Historical Atlas of South Asia*.

2

Ahura and Asura

Persians and Indians in the Time of the Buddha

THE BUDDHA LIVED and was active in the middle and lower Ganges plain around the sixth to the fifth centuries BCE, the very period when the Achaemenid Persian Empire ruled the north-west region of South Asia. The two political arenas were separated not only by the vast distance between the upper Indus and the Ganges, but also by the stronghold of Brahmanical culture in the Doab – roughly, the territory between the Indus and Ganges basins, a region that remained outside the urbanising trajectory of the mid-first millennium BCE. However, Brahmanical and Buddhist literature referring to the period from the sixth century BCE to the time of Ashoka Maurya shows that Taxila (Takshashila), the administrative site of the Persian satrapy in the Indian region, figures high as a centre of learning for all walks of knowledge among Indians living in the middle and lower Ganges. Meanwhile, asura – etymologically linked to the Persian word ahura, meaning gods in the Zoroastrian religion – had been evident in Indian literature for a very long time. On ritual occasions, asuras were considered supernatural beings who were somehow inferior to devas, the Vedic gods. In non-ritual contexts, asuras were mythical aliens, strangers, or outsiders. In the time of the *Satapatha Brahmana*, the Upanisads, and the Buddha, asuras represent both secondary deities that are sometimes hostile to devas in the Brahmanical cosmos, as well as foreigners coming in historically from the north-west. These latter human asuras were either agents of the Achaemenid regime, or else individual Persians who ventured out of their cultural domains and into Indian communities. It is also possible that there were enclaves of Zoroastrians who had settled in South Asia at various times and who kept to themselves, not mixing with Brahmanical society. In a word, for Indians these were "others", different from "us", though living around "us".

The Presence of the Persian Empire

Persian rule over north-west India (circa 519–327 BCE) is well documented.[1] But evaluation of the impact and legacy of the Persian regime is complicated by the fact that the Achaemenid Empire was a political entity embracing numerous cultural communities with several languages, occupying a vast geographic area of diverse landscapes and many cultural traditions, some of which dated back to remote antiquity. Therefore the impact of the Persian regime in north-west India was multifaceted and not something very singularly "Persian".

The most obvious impact of nearly two centuries of Achaemenid rule is that it installed the satrapy administrative system in India. The satraps were governors who supervised law and order and collected tributes, and meanwhile developed and maintained an infrastructure for production and trade, such as roads and currency. The Bhir Mound at ancient Taxila represents the only excavated archaeological remnant of Persian rule in South Asia. The sixth century BCE was when the Achaemenid kings started issuing gold and silver coins, a practice they had learned from Lydia (modern-day Anatolia) after conquering it. The Persian king Darius standardised royal coinage into gold daric and silver siglos. However, this royal coinage was not an imperial currency circulating across the

[1] See Hallock, *The Persepolis Fortification Tablets*. These tablets were written in Elamite and are dated to 509–494 BCE, during the reign of Darius I. My thanks to Suchandra Ghosh for this reference.

whole of his vast empire. It was made and used mostly in western Asia Minor, where a monetary economy already existed before the Persian arrival.[2] The Persian apparatus collected tributes from satrapies in gold dust, and the satraps of the empire issued coins in line with local needs. The satraps in Taxila seem to have issued punch-marked silver coins similar to those of the cities on the North Indian plains. Excavations at the Bhir Mound have revealed only one worn-down siglos, but many of the silver punch-marked coins issued locally were in the standard followed by the Persian siglos.[3] Therefore the monetary system in the Persian satrapies of India seems to have been similar to as well as different from that in the Ganges plain.

The Persians who built the Achaemenid Dynasty had come unlettered into Iran – they were a people who did not know writing. Like the Vedic people, they were Indo-European speakers from the Eurasian steppe. Once settled in their territory, the Achaemenid kings developed a new script in cuneiform for their language, Old Persian. This dynastic writing was intended also as a form of communication with their god Ahura Mazda, who is found inscribed on sacred monuments in the Pasargadae Pillar of Cyrus, and on Darius' victory panel at Bistun in Media (western Iran). Two ancient cuneiform languages, Elamite and Akkadian, are carved alongside Old Persian to communicate with subjects familiar with West Asian languages.[4] This trilingual effort could hardly have covered the requirements of administering the many satrapies of a great variety of cultures. More commonly for everyday needs, Aramaic – a Semitic tongue related to Hebrew and Phoenician – was the bureaucratic language and form of writing of the empire. Phoenicians had invented the earliest alphabets and used them for the Aramaic language, which had been the lingua franca of the traders of western

---

[2] Curtis and Tallis, *Forgotten Empire*, pp. 200–1.

[3] Marshall, *Taxila*, vol. I, 14, p. 106.

[4] Curtis and Tallis, *Forgotten Empire*, pp. 18–21. Assyria stretched over modern-day Iraq as well as parts of Iran, Kuwait, Syria, and Turkey.

Asia since 950 BCE.[5] It was also the language of diplomacy used in the confrontation between King Sennacherib of Assyria and Judah.[6] Aramaic eventually replaced Hebrew as the language of the Jews. After Cyrus returned Jews to their homeland – which was under the Persian Empire – Aramaic developed as one of the Persian languages. The ruling elite of the empire being illiterate in the ancient languages (and for that matter even in their own language), they had at least for the first couple of generations to employ scribes from trading communities, including the Jews, to assist their satraps in ruling their conquered territories. The official documents in the Persepolis Fortification and Treasury archives were written in Elamite, but there are references to "Babylonian scribes writing on leather" in Aramaic, these being different from Babylonian scribes writing Akkadian cuneiform on clay tablets.[7] Scribes from Mediterranean shores thus seem to have travelled all the way to the frontier satrapies of the empire, including to Gandara and Hindush in the Indian north-west. Their Aramaic – a phonetic script and language – was the first written language used by officials and traders in India till at least the time of the Mauryan Empire. When people there who spoke a variety of Prakrit employed the twenty-two alphabets – all consonants – to express their own languages, they had to add more characters and revise the existing ones to express sounds not known in Aramaic. Eventually, this practice gave rise to the first Indian script, Kharoshthi.[8] Aramaic scribes could thus be said to have made

---

[5] Ibid., *Forgotten Empire*, p. 21.

[6] Coogan, ed., *The New Oxford Annotated Bible*, pp. 1025–6. Judah corresponds to the area around modern Jerusalem.

[7] Henkelman, "Cyrus the Persian", pp. 577–634, 587.

[8] Many scholars of Indian epigraphy have studied and discussed the origins of the Kharoshthi script. Though their opinions on the transition from Aramaic to Kharoshthi vary, they largely agree that Kharoshthi derived from Aramaic. A brief summary is given in Konow, ed., *Kharoshthi Inscriptions*, pp. xiii–xv. A recent study is Glass, "A Preliminary Study of Kharoshthi Manuscript Paleography".

north-west India literate. It was this literacy that contributed to making Taxila a city of high culture.

The Persian Empire recruited soldiers from all ethnic communities, including Gandarans and Indians, into its huge army. As soldiers, Indians were not as trusted as the "immortals" – Persians, Medes, and Elamites. "The Indians wore garments made of tree-wool [cotton], and they had bows of reed and arrows of reed with iron points. Thus were the Indians equipped."[9] Herodotus, who noted this, was less impressed by their weapons than their cotton clothes. Military service to the Achaemenid Empire brought both Indians and their cotton – the unique Indian product in the ancient world – to West Asia, and to the notice of the Greeks. As subjects of the empire, Indians paid official tributes to the Persian kings. In the Apadana Palace at Persepolis (in modern Iran), a relief panel shows an Indian delegation with a well-dressed leader followed by barefoot dhoti-wearing delegates approaching the palace.[10] It is hard to guess the contents of the small jars they carry, they may have contained special or high-priced goods.

To garrison their vast empire and collect tributes, the Persian Empire built roads and maintained travel facilities. This enabled not only soldiers and officials, but also merchants from various satrapies to travel to lands they had probably never even heard of. Indians who fought in the Persian army and travelled to Persepolis and Susa for official duties will have brought back news and stories of the wonders they had encountered to their homeland, particularly to the satrapy's Indian headquarters at Taxila.

Zoroastrianism in Persia and India

The Achaemenids who inherited Zoroastrianism from their subjects made it the state religion and claimed their legitimacy from the god Ahura Mazda. However, the religion patronised by the Persian

---

[9] Herodotus, *The Histories*, VII.65, p. 369.
[10] Curtis and Tallis, *Forgotten Empire*, p. 67.

kings was quite different from the primary form of Zoroastrianism, which originated in the steppes of Central Asia. Zoroaster, the founder of Zoroastrianism, had created a doctrine deriving from a cosmology shared by Indo-Europeans on the steppes. In it the many deities of the universe belonged to two categories – benevolent Ahuras and warlike Daevas, these being synonymous with Indra and his followers. Ahura Mazda was the supreme original Ahura in this pantheon.[11] Zoroaster probably created his creed around the time when both Indo-Iranian and Indo-Aryan tribes were on the verge of entering sedentary lands, i.e. in the mid-second millennium BCE. This also meant creating a community to defend moral values and justice which were seen as lying on the side of Ahura Mazda. Those who followed this doctrine were to go to paradise after death, those against it would fall into hell.[12] In the centuries after Zoroaster, the community extended the doctrine with a set of rules about purity which supported their teacher's binary cosmos.[13] Water and fire were, in particular, the elements of purity, and various immoral things connected with Daevas were seen as polluting. Not everyone accepted Zoroaster during his own lifetime, but when the Indo-Iranian-speaking people settled in eastern Iran the community as a whole was largely Zoroastrian.

Having established Zoroastrianism as their state religion, the Persians built a religious institution of imperial grandeur around it. The superstructure required professional priests to perform rituals connected with claiming the legitimacy of their rule over newly conquered lands. The magus (pl. magi), professional priests from the Medes – long-time rivals who were also a neighbouring community before both entered Iran – took on the performance of rituals for the worship of Ahura Mazda, and for funereal rites. The image of Ahura Mazda that appeared on royal monuments was a winged circle, a symbol from Mesopotamia, which surrounded a figure in the style of Persian royalty.

[11] Boyce, *Zoroastrians,* pp. 20–1.
[12] Ibid., pp. 27–8.
[13] Ibid., pp. 43–6.

When Zoroastrians performed their sacrifices in Central Asia, their fire altars were positioned on open high ground. Under the Achaemenids, fire altars came to be established in palaces and became a sacred symbol of the regime.[14] At this time temples housing permanently burning fire altars came into being, possibly to counter temples housing the icons of other religions.[15]

The Persian kings were, all the same, ambiguous about these Zoroastrian funereal rites. Magi as well as ordinary Zoroastrians followed a purity rule which entailed leaving corpses to birds and dogs who would cleanse the body of its flesh to avoid polluting earth, water, and the skeletal remains that were to be buried. Kings and some of the nobility had their bodies placed in golden coffins which were set into excavated cave tombs on cliffs. Variations in Zoroastrian religious practices under the umbrella of the Persian Empire anticipated further ritual developments when Zoroastrianism spread further and encountered local cultic traditions in other regions.

When Gandara and Hindush became satrapies under the Persian Empire, Zoroastrians shared memories and even purity rules with Brahmanism – the ideological system of the Indo-Europeans who had migrated into South Asia. The universe of *Avesta*, which was the text of a dialogue between Ahura Mazda and Zoroaster, overlapped with that of the Vedas. The sacred "Harahvaiti" river in the *Avesta* is the Sarasvati of the Vedas.[16] "Hapta Hindu" (Seven Rivers) in the *Avesta* denotes the upper Indus basin.[17] The date of the *Avesta* is uncertain; it is probably later than the *Rg Veda*, which started to form around the mid-second millennium BCE. Meanwhile, both continued as oral traditions for many centuries. The religious codes of both had probably taken shape by the time the Achaemenids entered Punjab, denoting the Five Rivers – a region that was called "Sapta Sindhavah" (Seven Rivers) in the *Rg Veda*. Though their

[14] Ibid., p. 51.
[15] Ibid., p. 63.
[16] "Vendīdād", Fargard I, 13 (45), *The Zend-Avesta*, p. 7.
[17] Ibid., 19 (72), p. 9.

purity concepts contradicted each other's – i.e. the Zoroastrians considered Daevas (Persian for Devas) the ultimate polluting agents whereas the Brahmans saw Asuras as the representatives of evil forces – both Zoroastrians and Brahmans believed that a cow's urine was cleansing, a concept deriving from steppe life.[18]

The practices that most distinguished the two parties were funereal rites. Though the cleansing of corpses varied regionally, not defiling earth and water was a doctrine fundamental to Zoroastrianism, with violations attracting elaborate purification rituals and bodily punishment.[19] Brahmans in India were well aware of Zoroastrian funereal practices but interpreted them thus: "The gods [devas] drove out the Asuras, their rivals and enemies, from this world; whence those who are godly people make their sepulchres so as to not be separate [from the earth], whilst those who are of the Asura nature, the Easterns (*pracya*) and others (make their sepulchral mounds) so as to be separated (from the earth), either on a basin or on some such thing."[20] In general, Asuras remained a secondary group of deities in late-Vedic literature, their role in Vedic rituals being similar to that of Yakshas and rakshasas. The latter two were probably peripheral peoples indigenous to South Asia, referred to as "Easterns" in the *Satapatha Brahmana*. The text clearly stipulates a distinction in burial rules for Asuras, who, like other outsiders, do not deserve interment directly in the earth. Asuras in this context were thus followers of the Zoroastrian faith, one of the "others" distinguishable from "us". In the Upanisads both devas and asuras are celestial beings originating in a common ancestor, Prajapati. Their rivalries cause them to be hostile to each other.[21] Even so, the name "Asurayana" is listed in Vedic lineages, as recorded in the Upanisads.[22] This could be an indication that some

---

[18] Boyce, *Zoroastrians,* p. 43.
[19] *The Zend-Avesta,* pp. 66–74.
[20] *Satapatha Brahmana,* XIII Kanda, 8 Adhyaya, 2 Brahmana, 1, pp. 429–30.
[21] Bṛhadāraṇyaka Upaniṣad, I.3. 1–28, *Upaniṣads,* pp. 9–12.
[22] Bṛhadāraṇyaka Upaniṣad, 2.6.3; 4.6.3; 6.5.2, pp. 33, 72, 93.

Asura-related individuals joined Vedic societies through marriages. In brief, although the antagonism between Brahmanic rituals and Zoroastrian religious practices – in addition to geographical distance – separated Iranians and Indians, speakers of the two most closely related Indo-European languages seem to have travelled into each other's domains and even settled in them.

Persians in Greater Gandara

Persian imperial rule reconnected the two ideologically close cousins, and meanwhile brought in people of various ethnic backgrounds from the empire into India. There is evidence of knowledgeable individuals on the eastern side of the Hindu Kush being aware of the Persian Empire and of people from there. The presence of Achaemenid administration in the Greater Gandara region has been confirmed by a collection of Aramaic documents originating in Bactria (now Afghanistan, Uzbekistan, and Tajikistan). There are thirty documents inked on leather, plus eighteen documents on wooden tablets. Based on palaeography, one of the documents is dated to the fifth century BCE; the others have dates spread over 353–24 BCE. In other words, they were composed in the reigns of Artaxerxes III, Darius III, Bessos Artaxerxes [V], and Alexander the Great. Among the leather documents, eighteen are letters between a high Persian officer named Akhvamazda, and a governor of the city of Khulm (south of the Amu Darya in Afghanistan) named Bagavant. Their correspondence relates to state affairs, the military, and provisions. The wooden tablets were tailles – wooden sticks marking transactions. This private collection seems very possibly from the archive of either Akhvamazda, the satrap based in Bactria, or Bagavant, the governor of Khulm.[23] The name of the satrap suggests a Persian, while the governor Bagavant sounds Indian. The language of the documents is the same Aramaic found on Achaemenid documents in Egypt.[24] The authenticity of the documents is not in doubt.

[23] Shaked, *Le satrape*, pp. 13–14.
[24] Ibid., p. 22.

Panini, who composed the first Sanskrit grammar, was a later contemporary of the Buddha.[25] He was from Gandara, which was roughly the area of the Persian satrapies of Gandara and Hindush.[26] In his *Ashṭādhyāyī*, Panini refers to a polity, "Parshu", and to the people of that community as "Parshava", which he calls a "militant sangha" (*āyudhajīvi sangha*). Commentaries, probably added later, include Asuras and Balhika (Bactria) in the same category.[27] For Panini, Asuras were real people, as in the exemplary phrase "*Asurasya svam*" (belonging to the Asuras), and the comment "this vessel made on a wheel by a potter belongs to the Asuras."[28] The Asuras in this context were individuals, likely Zoroastrians, living in Panini's India.

That Panini, a person from Persian-ruled Gandara, composed Sanskrit scholarship from the perspective of the Brahmanical tradition says a lot about the cosmopolitan character of Gandara. In this region adjoining West Asia, Central Asia, and South Asia, Taxila was the hub of cultural and commercial flows. However, archaeological excavations at Bir Mound, the site at Taxila dating from Achaemenid rule to the Mauryan period, reveal no monumental buildings. This suggests a populous urban centre with residential buildings and public spaces. The civic planning is poor, with rudimentary drainage and pebble-paved roads in zigzags around houses.[29] Very early silver coins excavated in this part of India are in the Persian sigloi standard.[30] The Aramaic of the Persian

---

[25] There have been many discussions about the dates of Panini. According to the most recent research by George Cardona, "it is appropriate to say that Panini lived no later than the mid fourth century BC. In view of the state of the language that Panini describes, moreover, it is reasonable to consider that he may well have thrived as early as 500 BC." Cardona, "Panini's Dates", pp. 153–77, 167.

[26] Agrawala, *India as Known to Pāṇini*, p. 9.

[27] Ibid., pp. 447, 466; Chandra, ed., *The Ashṭādhyāyī of Pāṇini*, V.iii.117, p. 980.

[28] Ibid., IV.Iv.123, p. 843.

[29] See Marshall, *Taxila*, "Bhir Mound", vol. 1, pp. 87–111; "Plan of Excavations on the Bhir Mound", vol. 2, plate 2.

[30] Marshall, *Taxila*, vol. 1, pp. 106, 14–15.

bureaucracy was evidently in use in Taxila, continuing until at least Ashoka's stationing there as a Mauryan governor in the third century BCE. An inscription in Aramaic referring to "our lord Priyadarsi", i.e. Ashoka, has been understood as evidence that Ashoka was the viceroy at Gandara before he gained the throne.[31]

For all its connections with the Achaemenid imperial power in India, Taxila was a copy of neither Persepolis nor Susa. It was a prosperous and culturally polished city, absorbing talents and cultures from Persia, India, and Central Asia. When Alexander arrived in India in 327 BCE, Taxila city and its ruler, Taxiles, received his force in friendship and even joined hands in the invader's battle against Porus (Puru). Taxiles offered 3000 oxen and over 10,000 sacrificial sheep. Alexander duly performed various sacrifices to the gods – the meat was likely consumed by Alexander's soldiers – and held contests featuring athletics and horsemanship on the banks of the Indus.[32] The athletics and horsemanship contests were perhaps Greek military customs.

Alexander and the Greek writers of his time and later were puzzled by various phenomena that they observed in Taxila. The local sages there demonstrated feats of yoga, showing uncommon human endurance.[33] Some Greek writers believed there were two kinds of Brahmans to be found here – those who served the king as counsellors, and others who were engaged in studying the world of nature.[34] Alexander also tried to interact with a certain sect of Indian naked "wise men", but their leader rejected his patronage.[35] It was noted that the poor sold their daughters in the market, and widows in polygamous households joined deceased husbands on the cremation pyre. On the other hand, women also joined Brahman philosophers to study and live as ascetics.[36] Some of the Greek writers

---

[31] Ibid., pp. 164–5.
[32] Arrian, *The Campaigns of Alexander*, p. 259.
[33] Strabo, XV.1.61, in McCrindle, *Ancient India*, p. 68.
[34] Strabo, XV.1.66, in McCrindle, *Ancient India*, p. 72.
[35] Arrian, *The Campaigns of Alexander*, p. 350.
[36] Strabo XV.1.62, 66, in McCrindle, *Ancient India*, pp. 69, 72.

were impressed by the special Zoroastrian funereal rites of Taxila: "the dead are thrown out to be devoured by vultures".[37] The comment is evidence of Zoroastrians in Persian-controlled Gandara, and the existence therefore of possibly other immigrant communities as well.

Looking from the Ganges

From the perspective of the middle and lower Ganges, where the Buddha, Mahavira, and other challengers of the orthodox Brahmanical tradition were active, and where several polities vied for hegemony, it would seem that Taxila and the Gandara region – including the Persian satrapies of Gandara and Hindush – were rather distant even if distinguished places in the outer orbit of their culture. Apparently people in the Ganges plain were not aware of Taxila in Gandara being under a foreign regime, imagining it as some wonderful place located at the geographical periphery of the known world. Meanwhile, Taxila's repute for learning, especially Brahmanic learning, attracted numerous young elites to travel all the way there from the lower Ganges. The jatakas, a collection of stories in the frame of the former lives and contemporary deeds of the Buddha, frequently refer to such trips to Taxila for education. Most of the young people who made these educational tours were the sons of Brahmans and kings. Those whose families could afford tuition paid their teachers handsomely, and those not so well off paid via services to the teachers' households. Young Brahmans and princes studied the same variety of subjects, ranging from the Vedas, the Sanskrit language, martial skills such as archery, and magical charms.[38] In one curious case, a "Brahman" family in Benares practised fire worship at home and the mother sent her son to Taxila to study worship of the Lord of Fire.[39] Both Zoroastrians and Brahmans, as noted, practised fire worship: under the

---

[37] Strabo XV.1.62, in McCrindle, *Ancient India*, p. 69.
[38] *Jātaka Stories*, trans. E.B. Cowell.
[39] Ibid., Book I, no. 61, vol. I, pp. 147–50.

Achaemenids fire-altar worship had developed into an institution. This Brahman family in Benares could have been expressing a caste wish to learn the specifics of fire worship, or else it could have been a Zoroastrian immigrant family wishing to maintain their tradition.

The jatakas were Buddhist texts written in Pali, which, as noted earlier, had developed from Magadhi, the Prakrit language spoken in the Magadha region. The Buddha most likely spoke Prakrit as defiance of Brahmanical orthodoxy. Among the observations of Buddhists we find the view that, in the geo-political context of the Persian occupation of north-west India vis-à-vis the struggle for hegemony on the Ganges plain, Brahmans and princes had to get a Brahmanical education in Taxila to maintain their elite status. After their education, some of these young Brahmans pursued ascetic lives, often in the foothills of the Himalayas; others performed religious rituals for a living. Yet other young Brahmans were destined to be counsellors to kings: in cases of the last, the son of a Brahman adviser to the king and the king's heir apparent were raised and sent together to Taxila to learn statecraft.

One major reason that Brahmans and princes had to travel to Taxila for their education was possibly that Gandara was where they could learn a standardised Sanskrit. It was a time when Vedic Sanskrit was no longer adequate for the complicated social and economic conditions of urbanisation and state formation: the pioneering Gandara grammarian Panini had laid the foundations for a standardised Sanskrit. Subsequently, knowledge of this form of the language developed as the mark of educational status across the whole of North India.

A jataka story relates two young men, Citta and Sambhuta, of the Candala community of outcastes, aspiring to change their status and join the upper castes. Pretending to be Brahmans, they went off to Taxila to study under a teacher there. It so happened that, when eating a morsel of hot food, Sambhuta inadvertently uttered a phrase in their outcaste accent which betrayed their low birth, leading to their deportation from Taxila and subsequently to their becoming ascetics.[40] Even though Taxila had a culturally diverse environment, learning was still off limits in its Brahmanical schools for those of very low status.

It is possible that the Sanskrit language, regulated by clear grammatical rules, developed into a major component of Brahmanical orthodoxy in the region of the interface between the Zoroastrian and Vedic traditions. It was in Gandara after all that the Aramaic script, brought in by the Persian imperial administration and probably also traders, had been adapted to the local language and then evolved into Kharoshthi, South Asia's first alphabetically arranged writing system. There are no manuscripts of the original Panini texts, but Panini is likely to have used writing, instead of the oral tradition, to record his works. It is highly unlikely that he could have arrived at a highly technical narrative mnemonically within the oral tradition, especially as his grammar is a secular and not a sacred treatise requiring spoken dissemination. He could certainly have used Aramaic, which we know prevailed in his region till at least the third century BCE. However, the Aramaic script has only consonants and therefore could not record the complicated vowels of Sanskrit. It is also possible that he used and modified the Kharoshthi script for his written works. Kharoshthi alphabets do have vowels, but not long vowels; they are thus not adequate for the recording of complexities in Panini's complicated grammar. As a script only Brahmi is sophisticated enough for a Sanskrit grammarian, the modifications involving changes for the vocalisation of sounds being unique to Sanskrit. Furthermore, Brahmi runs from left to right, a rule followed by later Sanskrit texts. The problem remains that we have no direct evidence of Brahmi being used in Panini's time. As a symbol of high status, Sanskrit also became an avenue for people of low status to move up in the Brahmanical social hierarchy by acquiring knowledge of it. Citta and Sambhuta did not manage to make themselves Brahman priests, but they do not seem to have needed to go back to their status as untouchables: their ascent

---

[40] Ibid., Book XV, no. 498. vol. IV, pp. 244–6.

into Himalayan asceticism is also a social ascent along the lines of a Brahman template. Their travails suggest it cannot be ruled out that some young men of low caste did eventually climb the caste ladder to make successful careers in the military or the administration through study in Taxila. The success of any such transformation is more likely to have been kept under wraps than broadcast, and therefore not entering the historical record.

At the same time there were students from the Ganges area in Taxila studying for reasons other than acquiring knowledge of the Brahmanical tradition, and not all of them were Brahmans or princes. Their time in Taxila changed not only their careers but also introduced an element of larger social change. The best example of this is Jivaka, a physician who studied medicine at Taxila. He was an orphan abandoned by a courtesan at Rajagaha – boys being unwelcome in the matriarchal households of courtesans. The morning after his abandonment a prince discovered him on a trash heap and since he was still alive he was named Jivaka, meaning "alive". After learning all the medical knowledge available in Taxila, he returned to the lower Ganges region to establish himself as the best physician of his time. He treated everyone, high and low, and became physician to the Buddhist sangha. He advised the Buddha to establish standards of sanitation in the sangha, helping the sangha maintain healthy conditions in this early phase of urbanisation when epidemics were common.[41] The emphasis on a sanitary tradition certainly continued into later times within Buddhist communities.

Asuras Among the Buddhists

When creating a cosmology as the background to the Four Noble Truths, the Buddha largely accepted the hierarchy of a Brahmanical universe. In the cycles of rebirth, devas headed by Indra – often called Sakka in Buddhist terminology – occupy the highest and best place in the universe, excluding only the state of nirvana. The difference between the Buddhist universe and that of

---

[41] *Vinaya Texts*, Mahavagga, VIII.1–36, pp. 171–95.

the Brahmans is that in the former even the devas are subject to destiny and rebirth. Devas who live in the heavens owe their existing exalted lives to their virtue in previous lives. Once they have used up their accumulated merit, they fall out of heaven and must restart the process of moving up the universal ladder. The Buddha accepted that asuras were defeated by devas and chased out of heaven.[42] However, these asuras never appear as deadly foes of the Buddha – as does Mara.[43] Instead, asuras are included among followers of the Buddha: bhikkhus and bhikkhunis, lay brethren and lay sisters, devas and men, and asuras, Nagas, and Gandhabbas.[44] This list of followers shows a status hierarchy: the highest are members of the sangha, followed by lay followers who feed the sangha with alms. Then come devas and men, followed by asuras. Nagas were a cobra cult and Gandhabbas were celestial musicians. Creatures of sky and earth are listed together because the Buddhist cosmos is transient and dynamic.

The Nagas were, in my view, both a snake cult as well as a community outside mainstream society who worshipped the Naga cult.[45] The Asuras could, similarly, have been both the cult itself as well as worshippers of the Asura or Ahura, i.e. followers of Zoroastrianism living within India. The Buddhists despised certain religious practices of the community of "Kalakanjas Asuras", condemning them to an even lower status in the rebirth cycle than "Kora the Khattiya", who practised a hideous form of asceticism.[46] Asuras were, I believe, just another group of outsiders who "did not know better". The Buddhist attitude agrees with the Panini school of thought which puts asuras, rakshasas, and Balhikas (Bactrians), etc. under the category of Parsha – i.e. Persians.[47] The term denoted aliens living within the Indian domain.

[42] *Dialogues of the Buddha*, D.ii.207–9; idem vol. II, pp. 242–3.
[43] Ibid., D.iii.77, vol. III, p. 76.
[44] Ibid., D.iii, vol. I, p. 149; idem, vol. III, p. 142.
[45] Liu, "Naga and Dragon", pp. 183–97.
[46] *Dialogues of the Buddha*, D.iii.I, 7, vol. III, pp. 11–12.
[47] *The Ashtādhyāyī of Paṇini*, Bk V, Ch. III, § 117, p. 980.

"Asura", from this perspective, was the stereotypical name for various ethnic groups who came in from the Persian Empire, some of whom were settled in India for many generations and others who travelled to India for trade. The Persians who resided and travelled to the lower Ganges continued to follow their Zoroastrian traditions, which were strange and unsettling, perhaps at times even a bit threatening, in the minds of the local population. It is plausible to assert that it was for this reason that they were termed asuras after their own gods – the gods who were adversaries of the Vedic gods, the devas.

The presence and interaction of Asuras with local communities is clear from artwork on Buddhist monuments. On Stupa 1 at Sanchi, one of the earliest Buddhist monuments, a relief panel depicts a scene of Uruvela village – later Bodh Gaya – where the young Sakyamuni practices asceticism alongside various revelation seekers of his time (Fig. 1).

The narrative and themes of this panel have attracted much discussion because they show quite a few strange characters. The centre of the scene is a fire shrine, and a five-headed snake's hood over the fire seems to protect the fire. Seven figures who worship at the shrine wear distinctive hats and apparel not found in other figures at Sanchi. The only model for this kind of outfit appears in a delegation of Lydians shown on the Apadana Palace at Persepolis (Fig. 2).

Lydians were a major community in the western part of Iran and subjects of the Persian Empire, so it is possible that some Lydians reached India. However, their worship at a fire altar protected by a Naga cult needs more discussion and explanation in relation to the Sanchi panel by future scholars.

Another relief panel, also on Stupa 1, shows other kinds of foreigners worshipping a stupa (Fig. 3).

The worshippers' upper bodies are bare, their conical hats indicating they are Sakas from Central Asia. The higher temperatures in their new environment possibly made them take off their upper garment, their hats remaining as a mark of their ethnicity (possibly

Fig. 1: Uruvela Village. Sanchi Stupa 1, eastern torana, south pillar, north face. American Institute of Indian Studies, neg. no. 320.83, courtesy of the Library of the University of Pennsylvania.

Fig. 2: A member of Delegation VI, Lydians, on the east side of the Apadana Palace at Persepolis, author's drawing based on Curtis and Tallis, *Forgotten Empire*, plate 46, 106.

also functionally as resistance to the sun). Sakas were nomads from Central Asia who had entered the Persian Empire from the east. The Sakas here, obviously worshipping the Buddha, could have come either from Persian territory or from Central Asia.

Sanchi Stupa 1 was built in the reign of Ashoka. The relief panels on the railings surrounding the stupa were constructed in the decades after Ashoka and the Mauryan Empire. However, their stories may well reflect continuities or links from the time of the Achaemenids and the Buddha.

Fig. 3: Sanchi Stupa 1, foreigners worshipping a stupa, American Institute of Indian Studies, neg. no. 320.48, courtesy of the Library of University of Pennsylvania.

Two more stupas were built later by donors wishing to express their devotion through artwork. A scene showing a warrior fighting a lion on Stupa 2 is a strikingly Persian theme in a local artistic style (Fig. 4).

On the grand railing around the Bharhut Stupa, which is dated to soon after Sanchi in the Greater Magadha area, a more authentic Persian portrait stands on one of the pillars (Fig. 5).

These high-relief and human-size figures on all the major pillars are meant to be of named supporters of the Buddha. This was a

Fig. 4: Sassanid motif relief on Sanchi Stupa 2, ground balustrade, north entrance panel on pillar, American Institute of Indian Studies, neg. no. 24.7, courtesy of the Library of the University of Pennsylvania.

time when the Buddha could not be represented in images, and when supporters of the Buddha were revered in cults that followed the Buddha. The inscription pertaining to this particular majestic looking Persian figure says *bhadotamahilasa thabha dānaṁ*, meaning "Mahila gives the pillar to the Buddha". Here Mahila, the Pali form of Mathila, suggests a Persian name.[48] However, neither this

[48] *Bharhut Inscriptions*, A. 65, Plates XXXI, IX, pp. 40–1.

AHURA AND ASURA 47

Fig. 5: Bharhut Stupa, Persian patron, Indian Museum,
Calcutta, no. A24798, American Institute of Indian Studies,
neg. no. 244.69, courtesy of the Library of the University
of Pennsylvania.

figure nor the warrior fighting the lion on Sanchi Stupa 2 are portraits of Achaemenid royalty. Since the images were carved a couple
of centuries after the first Persian Empire, they could either embody
a recollection of the old glories of Persian immigrants, or else be
portraits of the donors themselves – of people who had travelled
to or settled in India closer to the time of the carvings.

The Persian occupation of India's north-west on the one hand, and urbanisation in the Ganges plain on the other, took place within the same time frame. Did the cities of the Ganges and those of the upper Indus learn and share knowledge of urban development? As a new phenomenon, cities absorbed all kinds of people, but they did usually maintain spatial distinctions between the established and newcomers, i.e. "us" and "them". Distinctions of class and caste were also inevitable in spatial arrangements: the riches of gahapatis and setthis – wealthy patriarchs – and the extreme poverty of outcastes kept them separate despite the more general prosperity of urban life. The Brahmanical tradition was still the orthodox cultural form, from Gandara in the north-west to Greater Magadha towards the south-east, but evidence of gradual social change and new worldviews and cosmologies is clear from the appearance of figures such as the Buddha. Persian imperial rule did not challenge the authority of the Brahmans, but it probably inspired some alterations in their religious practices – such as adding fire worship to their rituals. Asura / Ahura worshippers and Deva / Daeva worshippers continued to despise each other, but the voices of the Asuras were not obliterated and can occasionally be heard.

The implementation of writing for governance helped Indians to create their own script – Kharoshthi certainly, and possibly the Brahmi scripts. Writing also stimulated intellectual development outside of Brahmanic ritual. Panini from the Gandara area and Buddhists in the Ganges region brought greater literacy and a new literariness into society which challenged the Brahman monopoly of knowledge. Scholarship for non-ritual purposes, originating from Gandara, remained long after the retreat of the Achaemenids from there. Kautilya, the Mauryan scholar, and the Emperor Ashoka benefited from their sojourns in Taxila. Then there was Jivaka the physician who increased existing knowledge of medicine and created awareness of sanitation among Buddhists, a secular breakthrough of sorts inasmuch as it represented a departure from the mainly religious concept of purity in both the Brahmanical and the Zoroastrian traditions.

Persian occupation of the Greater Gandara region opened the Indian subcontinent to the Afro-Eurasian world. Indians were exposed, at least minimally and occasionally, to a variety of cultures from the eastern Mediterranean and Central Asia. People with a different style of clothing and religious practices managed to make their way in from various parts of the Persian Empire. Because Persians and Indians in the subcontinent's Indo-Gangetic stretch shared certain memories of a common ancestry, the Brahmanical and Buddhist traditions both conveniently categorised those practising Zoroastrian funereal rites as "Asura". The nomenclature served to distinguish Persians from the Yavanas, the Sanskritic version of Ionia, which denoted people from the Mediterranean region.

3

The Maladies of Urban Life

Epidemics, Asava, and the Problem of Addiction

THE NEW URBAN life on the Ganges meant abundant material wealth: people had not only more variety in their food, clothing, jewellery, and housing, but also more entertainment such as music and dance. City dwellers also encountered variety in the shape of different people who brought their culture into cities.

On the other hand, the maladies of urban society also threatened the pleasures of cultural life. Epidemics broke out from time to time; addiction to liquor, cannabis, and other intoxicants could cause social disorder and lead to family separations. Meanwhile, the Persian occupation of the Greater Gandara region opened South Asia to the cultures of Central Asia, West Asia, and even the East Mediterranean world. Taxila, as the governing centre of the Achaemenid satrapy of Hindush, became the hub of interactions for various religious communities who spoke Aramaic and other West Asian languages, and Sanskrit as well as a variety of Prakrit languages. Taxila could also impart knowledge of Brahmanical studies, Zoroastrian practices, statecraft, medicine, and secular knowledge and skills. It attracted students from the newly developed cities on the middle and lower Ganges. Brahmanical concepts of purity and pollution encountered the partly similar and partly different concepts of purity and pollution in Zoroastrianism. Secular concepts of sanitation and personal hygiene emerged from such cultural interactions.

The Buddhist sangha, scattered through cities and villages on the Ganges plain, built a community with clear disciplines which distinguished it from Brahmans and other Sramanas – i.e. unorthodox religious groups – and thus presented its lay supporters with a model lifestyle for reaching spiritual goals. A set of pollution-purity rules, implicitly contradicting those of the caste hierarchy, were created to guide bhikkhus and bhikkhunis to build a longer-lasting and more egalitarian community.

Jivaka the Physician in the New Cities

The new cities in the time of the Buddha, unlike the cities of the Harappa civilisation, started without urban planning for water supply and drainage; these were basically unplanned agglomerations. The building materials used were mostly clay and roughly cut rocks not suited to water ducts for a clean water supply or an underground drainage system. With the water supply varying from city to city, soakwells for sewage disposal were a common feature of early historical cities in South Asia. In the Bhir Mound, the best-excavated site of Achaemenid Taxila, the households all had private soakwells. Limited excavations at sites such as Kosambi also reveal soakwells in the form of unlined wells filled with pottery jars turned upside down, some with their bottoms knocked off, or lined with pottery rings commonly known to archaeologists as ring-wells.[1] With cities enticing and absorbing more and more people seeking their fortune within them, the primitive sanitation conditions were conducive to diseases which often expanded into epidemics.

Jivaka the physician was born in the Magadhan capital Rajagaha which was situated on the eastern edge of the Deccan Plateau. The communities here that were outside the Brahmanical tradition

---

[1] Ghosh, *The City in Early Historical India*, pp. 70–1.

supplied timber, elephants, and iron ore to the burgeoning cities and enlarging villages on the Ganges. Rice agriculture flourished and was an important item of merchandise for gahapatis and setthis, i.e. merchants, heads of artisan guilds, and financiers who comprised the nouveau riche. These were the supporters of the rulers of new regimes in kingdoms such as Magadha, and in oligarchical republic confederations such as the Vajji Ganasangha. Scribes, artists, musicians, dancers, and the entertainment professions formed guilds. Cities had prominent courtesans who were stars in their time. These were women skilled in music and dance who were also professional sex workers whose lives were organised within matriarchal households. New urban professionals from obscure backgrounds and uncertain lineages in these urban settings did not necessarily fit within the caste structure laid out by Brahmanism. Jivaka's mother Salavati, a courtesan at Rajagaha, entertained the king and citizenry, very likely individuals drawn from the elites who had commercial businesses in the city. All the same, when she became pregnant her pregnancy had to be kept hidden and eventually she abandoned the infant who was born, male children being something of a financial handicap within a household made up exclusively of earning women. Prince Abhaya, one of the sons of the king, Bimbisara, happened to see the infant on a dust heap where a murder of crows hovered. Realising the boy was alive, Abhaya had him plucked out and had Jivaka (meaning "alive") raised in his own household.[2] Apparently the adoption of abandoned infants by royalty was far from unknown at this time.

Jivaka realised that, for all the good fortune of his survival and early years, he needed to learn a skill to earn his livelihood. To this end he made a long trip to Taxila in the Persian satrapy of Hindush to study medicine, which he did under a famous physician for seven years. His story becomes more and more interesting. At his final exam, his teacher asked him to look around Taxila for plants that were of no medicinal use. The exercise was apparently

---

[2] *Vinaya Texts*, Mahavagga, VIII, I, 3–4, pt II, pp. 172–4.

intended to ensure that the examinee was able to clearly distinguish medicinal plants from those of no pharmaceutical value. Once his teacher had ascertained that Jivaka's botanical learning was sound, he gave him a little money and said he could go back home.

On his return journey Jivaka ran out of the money he had been given and so, when reaching Saketa, a major city in the Kosala kingdom, began using his newly acquired medical skill to earn the rest he needed to pay his fare. Hearing of a setthi's wife who suffered from a chronic headache and who had not been cured despite being treated by many physicians, Jivaka managed to persuade the woman to let him have a go. He prepared medicine by mixing various drugs in a cup of ghee which he boiled so that it absorbed the drugs. He then cooled and ministered the medicine via the woman's nostrils, allowing it to flow out through her mouth.[3] Recovered, the lady and her family rewarded Jivaka handsomely, his recompense including a male servant, a female servant, and a horse-drawn coach. With this first medical success of his career in the bag, Jivaka reached Rajagaha with something of a retinue. It seems that he had acquired knowledge of a large repertoire of medicinal plants during his training in Taxila, and by the time he reached the Ganges region his baggage included a veritable pharmacopoeia.

He offered the wealth he had earned at Saketa to his foster father as repayment for years of royal nurture. Ever generous, his father refused the money, instead retaining his foster son in the household and enlisting his services for the better health of the royal family, the residents of Rajagaha, and most important the Buddha and his sangha. Jivaka went on to cure King Bimbisara of a fistula by administering an ointment; the problem was not life-threatening but embarrassing all the same. A grateful king, now more easily seated, named Jivaka physician of the royal household and of the Buddha's sangha.

Soon, influential setthis who had fallen sick had to plead with the king to allow Jivaka to treat them. When performing surgery on

---

[3] *Vinaya Texts,* Mahavagga, VIII, I, 8–13, pp. 176–9.

the head of a setthi to extract two subcutaneous parasitic worms, Jivaka had to tie the patient fast to his bed, there being no form of anaesthesia in those days. After the surgery, he applied medicinal paste to the wound to facilitate healing. Jivaka persuaded the patient to lie fixed first on one side and then the other and then on his back for seven days before leaving his bed.[4] The descriptions of the medical treatment are vivid and suggest that medical advances at the time of the Buddha had taken a path away from belief in religious rituals as ameliorative, and from witchcraft as the route out of illness.

Treating the powerful meant a good income but was a double-edged sword as kings were often suspicious of physicians: herbs could be medicinal or poisonous and were at best unpalatable. Pajjota, the king of Ujjeni (Ujjayini), suffered from a jaundice which many physicians could not cure, so he asked Bimbisara to depute Jivaka to help, and the physician proceeded to Ujjeni. However, Pajjota refused the medical compound he was prescribed as it included ghee, to which he was allergic. The problem for Jivaka was that the ghee wasn't merely the colloidal medium, it was one of the ingredients necessary for the cure. So Jivaka decided to disguise the taste of ghee and made what needed to be swallowed a stringent decoction which he knew would make the king vomit – a necessary step in the process of curing the disease. But a king who is made to vomit is unlikely to see the administering physician as one who is only being cruel to be kind. Fearing for his life, Jivaka made haste out of Ujjeni fairly quickly after giving medicine to the king. This proved prescient, for Pajjota, far from taking kindly to the potion, grew livid enough to want Jivaka killed. Subsequently, matters took a turn for the better and the king of Ujjeni gained his health. Jivaka, being understandably hesitant to revisit Ujjeni and be paid for services rendered, was sent a robe of fine cloth as payment by Pajjota.[5] Sending Jivaka to Ujjeni had been meant as

---

[4] Ibid., VIII, I, 16–20, pp. 181–4.
[5] Ibid., VIII, I, 23–9, pp. 186–91.

a goodwill gesture by Bimbisara, but the Ujjeni king's repute for cruelty had not been sufficiently kept in mind. Jivaka was lucky to have made his way back to Magadha in one piece, and to have received a magnificent robe in the bargain.

Jivaka believed that the only person really deserving a robe as glorious as the one given to him was the Buddha, and he found an opportunity to present it to the sage when the venerable one suffered what was probably a skin infection. After treating the Buddha with several kinds of medicine and ointments as well as a warm bath, Jivaka presented the robe to him, saying:

> Lord, the Blessed One wears only *paṁsukūla* robes [made of rags from a dust heap or cemetery] and so does the fraternity of Bhikkus. Now, Lord, this suit of *Seveyyaka* cloth has been sent to me by King Pajjota, which is the best, and the most excellent, and the first, and the most precious, and the noblest of many cloths and of suits of cloth, and of many hundred suits of cloth, and of many thousand suits of cloth, and of many hundred thousand suits of cloth. Lord, may the Blessed One accept from me this suit of *Seveyyaka* cloth, and may he allow to the fraternity of Bhikkhus to wear robes fit for householders (*gahapaticivara*).[6]

Jivaka was, it seems, using the occasion to advise the Buddha as well as the entire sangha to abandon their dirty and ragged apparel and instead accept the clean clothes donated them by decently clad lay followers. When the Buddha and the sangha received new clothing from the laity, rules were framed to distribute the material and a dress code for all came into effect. Jivaka's advice reportedly initiated a process for the wearing of robes by monks which has evolved but also persisted all the way into our own time, the textile varying according to climate and cultural environment.

Jivaka worked gratis, serving the Buddha and the sangha well. When the "five contagious diseases, leprosy, boils, dry leprosy, consumption, and fits" prevailed in Magadha, Jivaka had to take care of the royal family and the Buddhist sangha and had little time left

[6] Ibid., VIII, I, 30–4, pp. 191–4.

to tend to non-Buddhist patients. Some of these therefore decided to join the sangha in order to be treated by Jivaka and cared for by bhikkhus. Many of the sick were ordained into the sangha, which exhausted the resources of the sangha. Bhikkhus had to solicit more food and medicine to maintain the prescribed standards, and Jivaka grew so busy that at times he neglected care of the royal family. A patient was discovered to have joined the sangha just for the duration of his cure and to have left the sangha soon after he had been cured. Jivaka berated this opportunist when he ran into him and reported his perfidy to the Buddha, asking that sick people wishing to be ordained be denied entry before they had been cured. To this the Buddha agreed, making it the rule that the diseased not be officially ordained into the sangha.[7] Preventing those who were sick from joining the sangha meant preventing them carrying contagion and disease into the sangha. Giving priority to the well-being of the sangha meant acknowledging that there were limits to the medical facilities that could be offered, and in this too Jivaka showed sagacity.

Health Conditions: Personal Hygiene and Environmental Sanitation

The medicinal materials Jivaka used were mostly from plants, as his training in Taxila shows. As for the specific plants used, this remains a good question. Over the period that members of the sangha had no permanent residence and ate one meal a day which they obtained as alms by going door to door, they inevitably fell sick because of the harsh weather, malnutrition, and infections. This meant that the Buddha and his followers often had to resort to a variety of remedies, with bhikkhus and bhikkhunis needing health guidelines. One story, pertaining to a time when the Buddha stayed at Jetavana – a garden donated to the sangha by a famous elder, Anathapindika in the city of Savatthi – reveals the nature of some of the medical problems of the day. The monks accompanying the

---

[7] Ibid., I, 39, 1–7, pt 1, pp. 191–4.

Buddha suffered heat exhaustion, resulting in their throwing up the rice and milk they had eaten. Many were dehydrated and suffered fatigue. For them the Buddha's prescribed remedy was ghee, butter, oil, honey, and molasses.[8] These five ingredients were believed to not only provide basic nutrition but also a base for herbal ingredients to be mixed into a medicine easily digested. Though all five ingredients were relatively resistant to decay, the Buddha had guidance to offer on their shelf-life: they had to be used within seven days and discarded thereafter.[9] The injunction suggests a keen awareness of the local tropical climate's effect on perishable items of food, and about food poisoning.

We also know that a remedy for snakebite was made of cow dung, urine, ashes, and clay. This was a decoction that had to be drunk to overcome the poison.[10] Such uses of cow dung and urine were likely common remedies of the time. The ammonia present in a cow's urine, and urine in general, was reckoned as helpful in suppressing certain germs and poisons.

The Buddha did not encourage extreme asceticism; thus, he allowed monks to use not only plants but also animal fat and perfumes in the making of healing ointments, and even pig's blood if the illness required, and fruit drinks and meat broth when malnutrition was the problem.[11] Certain diseases were believed to require a strong drink, including alcohol in medicinal oil. If there happened to be a surplus of alcohol-based medicine, the Buddha instructed his monks to use it as skin ointment against dermatitis. In the treatment of skin ailments medicinal herbs, including hemp water or cannabis (*bhang*) were used.[12]

To keep the sangha in good health, certain general rules were meant to apply to all monks. When Jivaka noticed that the bhikkhus at Vesali (Vaishali), the capital of the Vajji Ganasangha,

[8] Ibid., VI, I, 1–2, pt II, pp. 41–2.
[9] Ibid., VI, 15, 10, pt II, pp. 66–7.
[10] Ibid., VI, 14, 6, pt II, p. 59.
[11] Ibid., VI, 10, 2, pt II, 49; VI, 14, 7, pt II, pp. 60–1
[12] Ibid., VI, 14, 2–3, pt II, pp. 56–7.

seemed bloated with eating too many sweetmeats given them by their patrons, he advised the Buddha to have an area (Cankama) levelled for monks to exercise in, and bathrooms in which to bathe.[13] The Buddha heeded this advice, which went a long way in making the sangha a model of the healthy life. To further their personal hygiene, the Buddha advised that there were "five disadvantages, O, bhikkhus, in not using tooth-sticks – it is bad for the eyes – the mouth becomes bad-smelling – the passages by which the flavours of the food pass are not pure – bile and phlegm get into the food – and the food does not taste well . . ."[14] The origins of the practice of teeth hygiene in this region of the world may well lie in the guidelines established in the time of the Buddha. The Chinese monk Yijing, who travelled to India (671–85) to gather monastic rules for the Chinese Buddhist monasteries, stipulated in detail how teeth were to be cleaned. Buddhist monks should clean their teeth with *dantakāṣtha* – meaning "teeth wood". The user must choose a soft twig a few inches long and flatten one end of it to clean the teeth and tongue. Some species of trees were preferred for the smell and cleansing effect of the twigs used.[15] More than a thousand years after the Buddha, Buddhist communities, regardless of their specific branch of Buddhism, continued with this dictum on oral hygiene.

Drugs as Medicine and Addiction

Prescribing a healthy lifestyle could not, naturally, resolve the problem of certain maladies among members of the sangha. Many bhikkhus and bhikkhunis joined the sangha to escape the hardships and difficulties of quotidian life, so addiction to intoxicants such as alcohol and drugs for pain were far from unknown. In the

---

[13] *Vinaya Texts*, Kullavagga, V, 14, 1, pt III, pp. 102–4.

[14] The implement to clean teeth was a soft twig or piece of creeper with the end knocked loose. This has been used by Buddhists for many centuries. *Vinaya Texts*, Kullavagga, V, 31, 1–2, pt III, pp. 146–8.

[15] Yijing, *Nanhai Jiguinei Fa Zhuan Jiaozhu*, pp. 44–5.

Theragatha and *Therigatha* – collections of psalms composed by senior monks and nuns – many authors speak of how they had first to rid themselves of asava (defilements; cankers) in order to reach the peace of mind to which Buddhists aspired.

This brings us to what exactly asava indicates, a word which became the topic of much discussion among Pali scholars. The term has been translated variably as "drugs", "cankers", "intoxicants", or left untranslated to be understood by its contextual usage since it embodied a spectrum of meaning – this was T.W. Rhys Davids' preference in his translation of *Sabbasava Sutta* (All the Asavas). According to this Pali text, there are four categories of asava: kama (passion), bhava (being alive), avijja (ignorance), and ditti (delusion).[16] The word asava is found only in Pali Buddhist texts. When the word was Sanskritised into asrava in the Mahayana texts a few centuries later, its meaning changed. The general consensus has tended to be in favour of interpreting asava as an urgent and specific issue concerning mental conditions during the Buddha's time.

In his discussion of asava the Buddha considered three fetters that constrained human life – delusions about the self (atma), hesitation, and dependence on rites and ceremonies. These were seen to prevent those who suffered from the cessation of suffering. These three fetters seem to have been closely connected to the remedies offered by Brahmans and other ritualistic sects of the day. The Buddha, however, saw these remedies as asava, things that needed to be abandoned in view of his own insight, which was expressed as the Four Noble Truths, namely the analysis of suffering, the origin of suffering, the cessation of suffering, and the way towards the cessation of suffering. Another way to be rid of asava was by subjugation (*samvara*), i.e. by closing off one's sight, hearing, smell, taste, touch, and thought processes, a prescription for solitary meditation intended to cut out all stimulation from the environment. Meanwhile, to stay alive and healthy, the correct use (*patisevana*) of asava was also a means for getting rid of asava. For instance, though

---

[16] *Sabbasava Sutta*, pp. 293–5.

robes were a form of material wealth, it was the right thing to wear robes to stay warm in cold weather and keep cool in hot weather, it was right to fend off flies and mosquitoes and snakes, and it was right to cover one's nakedness with clothing. Accepting alms and shelter, and consuming the right medicines for illness and injury, were other recommended ways of using asava to get rid of asava. Yet other remedies for asava included the enduring of hardships, avoiding dangerous situations, removing sinful impulses such as lust, hatred, and anger, and the cultivation of character towards higher forms of wisdom.[17]

In this particular monologue the Buddha obviously does not equate asava with suffering or the origin of suffering; rather, he seems to designate asava as a hindrance to the cessation of suffering. Among the recommended remedies, the correct use of asava to counter asava is an attempt to reach a compromise which would resolve the contradiction between asavas as, on the one hand, facilitators of desire for material goods, and on the other as the material necessities for remaining alive and pursuing enlightenment.

Though the use of medicine to treat illness and injury was a beneficial use of asava, the problem remained that medicines against pain could be addictive. The reasons for taking recourse to drugs were plentiful, given the difficulties of dealing with the challenges of urban life. Social upheavals seem to have been frequent in this period, with some individuals gaining great wealth overnight and others losing everything suddenly, and some venturing successfully into the urban sphere even as others were cast out of it. In these circumstances, drugs and intoxication could seem major assets to people having to cope with life's many vicissitudes. Opium was known to ease physical pain and many opiates or palliative drugs used against illnesses came to be used addictively.

Among those addicted to drugs in the early cities were courtesans who provided sex services and entertainment to urbanites with their skill in music and dance. These courtesans were outsiders

[17] Ibid., pp. 301–6.

who did not have the usual protection of family networks, their compensation being that they could become famous and wealthy. A woman named Vimala was a courtesan in the city of Vesali. It was said that she tried but failed to seduce Maha-Moggallana, one of the Buddha's foremost disciples. The reason Vimala tried to entice a famous disciple of the Buddha was perhaps that she saw it as the best opportunity to enhance her fame as an entertainment star. After she failed in this, she joined the sangha in a state of shame:

> How was I once puff'd up, incens'd with the bloom of my beauty,
> Vain of my perfect form, my fame and success 'midst the people,
> Fill'd with the pride of my youth, unknowing the Truth and unheeding!
> Lo! I made my body, bravely arrayed, deftly painted,
> Speak for me to the lads, whilst I at the door of the harlot
> Stood, like a crafty hunter, weaving his snares, ever watchful.
> Yea, I bared without shame my body and wealth of adorning;
> Manifold wiles I wrought, devouring the virtue of many.
> Today with shaven head, wrapt in my robe, I go forth on my daily round for food;
> And 'neath the spreading boughs of forest tree
> I sit, and Second-Jhana's rapture win,
> Where ras'nings cease, and joy and ease remain.
> Now all the evil bonds that fetter gods
> And men are wholly rent and cut away.
> Purg'd are the Asavas that drugg'd my heart,
> Calm and content I know Nibbana's Peace.[18]

Vimala withdrew from the courtesan world at the peak of her career to seek tranquillity in the sangha. Even though no specific details are provided regarding her asava, she seems to have released herself from an addiction to drugs which may have been essential for success within her profession. Their entertaining activities, such as dancing and singing, demanded much energy, and the drugs were perhaps quite essential as stimulants. The entertainment business

---

[18] *Therigathā*, XXXIX, pp. 52–3.

that Vimala was engaged in was the main path to glory in her urban culture, but hers was also a low-status profession within the Brahmanical social structure. Joining the sangha meant a decent retreat into retirement, seclusion, and de-addiction.

Those of high status in the Brahmanical hierarchy were not exempt from a sudden and precipitate fall into the social abyss. A woman named Canda, born in a Brahman family in a Brahman village, grew up over a time when her family were impoverished, and then she had the misfortune to see epidemic disease wipe out all her relatives. When Canda was doing her rounds begging for food, she encountered bhikkhunis begging for alms and joined them:

> Fallen on evil days was I of yore.
> No Husband had I, nor child, nor friends,
> Or kin – whence could I food or raiment find?
> As Beggars go, I took my bowl and staff,
> And sought me alms, begging from house to house,
> Sunburnt, frost-bitten, seven weary years.
> Then came I where a woman Mendicant
> Shared with me food, and drink, and welcomed me,
> And Said: "Come forth into our homeless life!"
> In gracious pity did she let me come –
> Patacara – and heard me take the vows.
> And thenceforth words of wisdom and of power
> She spake, and set before my face
> The way of going to the Crown of Life.
> I heard her and I marked, and did her will.
> O wise and clear Our Lady's homily!
> The Threefold Wisdom have I gotten now.
> From deadly drugs my heart is purified.[19]

Patacara was a senior bhikkhuni who had been saved by the Buddha himself when she had been in an extremely miserable and mentally broken state. She had then recruited many suffering women, including Canda. A young woman of high birth roaming

---

[19] Ibid., XLIX, pp. 75–6.

the streets and begging was clearly in need of relief from the daily grind – which she found in drugs; in her case, asava may have meant the substance she took to calm her mind. Patacara offered her a new approach to face the sufferings of life, even if it meant continued begging of food from door to door, the main difference being that by joining the sangha Canda could put on a robe signifying her status as a Buddhist nun and thereby acquire the more exalted trappings of a recognised order.

Among the early followers of the Buddha were quite a few Brahmans with no obvious maladies making them seek refuge. These were the souls who had sought out the sangha for the mental peace and tranquillity available by joining it. A bhikkhu named Ujjaya was one such accomplished Brahman scholar from Rajagaha. Though immersed in knowledge of three of the Vedas, he had failed to find happiness. He therefore went to Venavana, a bamboo grove near the city of Rajagaha, to listen to the Buddha. He was enlightened by what he heard and had this to say:

> Buddha the Wake, the Hero hail! All hail!
> Thou who from every bond art wholly free!
> Strong in the lore I learnt of thee, I live
> From fourfold venom cleansed, sane, immune.[20]

The fourfold asava in his poem sounds like a statement on asava in general, and not to any specific drug. However, Ujjaya was a Brahman, and Brahmans were consumers of soma, a drug used in rituals. The asava that made him feel insane before he joined the sangha sounds like Brahmanical rituals that included the consumption of soma. The early development of the soma cult shows only Brahman priests availing of this drink at rituals which included the process of extracting soma from plants. Whether or not he performed these rituals as a priest, Ujjaya certainly had experienced the effects of soma – which he did not like. Frits Staal, the famous scholar on Vedic rituals, observes that soma was a psychoactive plant revered

---

[20] Ibid., XLVII, pp. 52–3.

as a god by the Vedic people and ritualised around 1000 BC, when their socio-political centre was in the Kuru region, i.e. the Doab of the Indus and Ganges. As their terrain was much further away from the high mountains of the original soma plants, the priests had to moisten and swell the dry plants before pressing out the required substance.[21] The Buddha was staunchly opposed to Brahmanical rituals as the cure for *any* malady – which would have meant, *ipso facto*, his opposition to soma. The further the location of the Vedic ritual performed from high mountains, the harder for the priests to obtain the original soma. Substitutes of soma thus had to come into play. Whatever the true composition of soma by the time of the Buddha, it was addictive, and the use of soma had spread outside ritual occasions. Staal says: "We are puzzled by the not infrequent case of a drug addict overcoming addiction by religious conversion . . . Meditating daily for 10 hours may appear to be an addiction, but isn't that what Buddha did?"[22] So it seems there were at least some Brahmans who perceived the Buddhist sangha and the daily practice of meditation as a de-addiction therapy, and perhaps in the longer term as a rehab facility.

Soma, Haoma, Asava

What exactly were the asavas this Brahman scholar tried to get rid of in order to achieve a clear state of mind? And what sorts of drugs did sufferers use to ease their pain? Many kinds of intoxicants and stimulants were available in the early cities of South Asia. Alcohol and drugs, indigenous or imported from Persia and Central Asia, were probably easily procured. One of the apparent intoxicating sources of pain relief was soma in Brahmanical rituals and haoma in Zoroastrian sacrifices. This was a time when the Brahmans lost their monopoly of power as sole communicators with the gods, as well as when soma as a substance inducing hallucination moved out of its constrained use by Brahman priests during sacrificial occasions.

---

[21] Staal, "How a Psychoactive Substance Becomes a Ritual", p. 772.
[22] Ibid., pp. 772–3.

The early Brahmanical dharma literature appeared around the mid-first millennium BCE, probably in response to the rise of Buddhism and other challenges to Brahmanical orthodoxy. In the dharma text assigned to Gautama – the earliest known Dharmasastra – there are seven kinds of soma sacrifices, though the role of soma in the rituals is not designated.[23] Gautama says that if a person did something that was ritually polluting, one path to cleanse the body of sin was the performance of ascetic penance. These self-punishments included living only on milk, vegetables, and fruits, and drinking soma.[24] Soma was therefore seen as auspicious in sacrifices and effective in purifying the body. In another dharma text the sage Vasistha declared that Brahmans and Ksatriyas who could not survive through their usual methods of making a living could resort to the Vaisya's way of living, but that they should not sell certain forbidden stuffs, including soma; nor should they accept food given by a soma plant seller.[25] From this it would seem that soma, despite having become a commodity, was associated with sellers of low and polluting status.

Manu, the classical dharma author a few hundred years later, discusses soma in a different way. When agreeing with Vasistha that Brahmans and Ksatriyas resorting to the Vaishya's way of making a living should not sell soma and other forbidden materials, Manu speaks of those who were qualified to drink soma for purification purposes. The twice-born man who possesses wealth enough to support a family for three years is qualified to drink soma juice, whereas the less affluent can get no benefit from drinking soma.[26] This ruling also indicates that soma was addictive enough to bankrupt a well-to-do Brahman, so that only those with sufficient financial reserves should consume it. The use of soma seems to have spread far beyond ritual occasions – enough to have plagued Brahmans or even the whole of society.

[23] Gautama, *Institutes of the Sacred Law*, VIII, 20, p. 217.
[24] Ibid., XIX, 13, p. 276.
[25] *Vasistha Dharmasastra*, pt II, 26, p. 12; pt XIV, 3, p. 69.
[26] *Laws of Manu*, X, 88, pp. 420–1; XI, 7, 8, p. 432.

Some of the asavas referred to in the psalms of senior brothers and sisters in the Buddhist sangha could be soma, the very drink used by Brahmans in their ritual sacrifices to the gods. But what precisely was soma? The hallucinogenic drink was, according to the procedure given for its production in Vedic literature, a juice pressed from a plant. Numerous scholars have tried to identify the plant. Because Vedic culture and Avestan culture shared a common ancestry in Central Asia, and Zoroastrian rituals speak of the use of haoma – a word that shares its Indo-European etymology with soma – research on soma has often been combined with that on haoma. Archaeological discoveries and literary references to both substances have focused on Central Asia. While there is no single conclusive answer which pins down a specific plant as soma / haoma, discussions suggest that there could have been several plants used by these communities for religious and medical purposes, and that both soma and haoma could have been different drugs in different regions and time periods. An article by the Uzbek scholar Kazim Abdullaev points out the complexity of the issue and summarises archaeological evidence from the regions of Margiana, Bactria, and Sogdiana for the various plant candidates of these sacred drugs. The candidate plant-drugs for haoma found in Central Asia, he says, are ephedra, opium, and cannabis. A nomadic people named Saka Haomavarga, or the Saka of Haoma in Persian imperial inscriptions, were subjugated by Cyrus of the Achaemenids.[27] Under Achaemenid imperial rule haoma was used routinely in the worship of Ahura Mazda. The components of the ritual substance could have been a compound of ephedra, opium, and cannabis, or possibly one or two of these drugs blended with sweeteners. All of them show stimulant effects as well as medical benefits.

Focusing on soma in the context of South Asia, Harry Falk identifies ephedra as the drink used in Vedic rituals. Various ephedra species are called hum, hom, some, or soma in a large geographical area from Herat to the Indian Himalaya. Even till today

---

[27] Abdullaev, "Sacred Plants and the Cultic Beverage Haoma", pp. 129–40, 132.

the Parsis – the Zoroastrians of India – use ephedra as their sacred haoma drink.[28]

From the time of the Bronze Age in Central Asia, as early as the third or second millennium BCE, the peoples of the Central Asian oases and those that roamed the steppes used these plants for pain suppressants and more generally as yielding potent antidotes to their harsh climatic conditions. Archaeologists have long noticed that in ancient burials the dead are often clutching ephedra in their departure to the next world. In more recent decades, excavations in the eastern part of Central Asia have shown that using ephedra started long before the coming of either Zoroaster or the Vedic priests. The archaeologist Wang Binghua excavated forty-two graves in a cemetery, Gumu Gou, located to the south of the Tianshan Range, and found that each of those buried roughly 4000 thousand years ago had attached to them a small woollen bag with ephedra twigs.[29] It would seem that ephedra was the most widely used drug in Central Asia and adjacent West and South Asia, as well as for the longest known period of time.

Haoma, consumed by the Zoroastrian priests, used ephedra as its major if not its only component. We have already noted that the Persian occupation of the Greater Gandhara region around the sixth to fourth centuries BCE brought Zoroastrianism to the northwest of the Indian subcontinent, and possibly even to the Ganges plains. Whatever the ingredients of the soma / haoma, the asava of the Buddha and his followers could have carried the same drug ingredients as soma / haoma. It must also be borne in mind that new substances of an intoxicating, stimulating, and addictive character proliferated and became more easily procurable with the vigorous commercial economy that characterised early urbanisation in the North Indian plains. Exotic alcoholic drinks such as grape wine could have been imported here through the satrapies of the Achaemenids. Another common drug of the time, cannabis, was derived from hemp, the popular plant used in the production of

---

[28] Falk, "Soma I and II", pp. 77–90, 84, 85.
[29] Wang, Binghua, Gumugou (Valley of Ancient Graves), pp. 41, 173.

fibre for textiles in many parts of Asia. The word for cannabis in ancient India, bhanga, has merely been shortened to bhang in modern times. In the *Vinaya* texts the Buddha allows bhanga water as a drink in the treatment of the rheumatism of a senior monk. The effect of the treatment not being clear, the Buddha instructs the use of a hot bath in which medicinal herbs have been steeped.[30] The herbs in the hot bath could conceivably have included bhanga. Cannabis, like ephedra, has been a medicinal drug with a long history of experimentation in South Asia.

A recent archaeological discovery on the Pamir Plateau verifies that a Zoroastrian ritual using cannabis was performed at the junction of Central Asia and Afghanistan approximately 2500 years ago. From the Jirzankal Cemetery here, archaeologists have recovered wooden braziers containing burnt rocks and residues. They have identified the wooden braziers as fire altars of Zoroastrian rituals associated with burials – both primary and secondary burials. The primary burials yielded no evidence of cloth, suggesting the corpses were buried naked. The secondary burials contained cleansed bones that were apparently buried after a period of exposure.[31] This burial method is not identical with Zoroastrian interment principles as known in the community's later literature, but it is in line with the concept of cleansing the skeleton of all flesh before putting the body into its final resting place. The burial goods found included carnelian beads, some of them etched with patterns (Plates 30, 32, 33, 35); agate beads, some etched (Plates 31, 34, 36); bone beads (Plate 68); numerous glass beads, including dragonfly eye beads (Plates 70, 71, 72, 73); silk; combs; and copper ware.[32] A wooden musical instrument, probably an angular harp (konghou, Plate 60) was positioned for service by the dead to enhance their appeal to the gods. No matter who the burials are of in the Jirzankal Cemetery in these high mountains, the buried were well connected with the world beyond their own area.

---

[30] *Vinaya Texts*, Mahavagga, VI, 14, 3, pp. 56–7.
[31] Wu Xinhua and Tang Zihua, "Jirzankal Cemetery", pp. 5–82, 41–2.
[32] Ibid., p. 40.

Chemical analyses prove that the residue on the braziers in the Jirzankal Cemetery was from burnt cannabis with high levels of psychoactive effects. This high concentration of psychoactive elements could have been from plants found at high altitudes, or through human selection and domestication. "We can start to piece together an image of funerary rites that included flames, rhythmic music, and hallucinogen smoke, all intended to guide people into an altered state of mind." In Jirzanka, cannabis altars have been associated with people of varying social status, indicating that the ritualistic smoking of cannabis was popular among people and not restricted to shamans.[33] This happened around 500 BCE, when the Persian Empire occupied the region west of the Pamirs, including Afghanistan and Gandara, and when the Buddha was preaching to people near the Ganges on how they might rid themselves of asava.

Asavas, whether ephedra or cannabis or other addictive plant sources with medical effects, seem to have flooded the newly urban cultures sprouting in the Ganges plains and were available to people with the means to purchase them. No wonder many bhikkhus and bhikkhunis claimed to have overcome asava when regaining mental tranquillity. From this perspective it becomes easier to understand that Buddhist food taboos included not only a bar on meat because it involved violence against a living creature, but also fermented or strong varieties of food that could serve as stimulants. At the same time, a large section of the *Vinaya* texts is devoted to remedies for illnesses that allow sick monks to consume foods banned in normal circumstances.[34] Bhang may well have been one of these.

As addiction was such a serious social problem in society and the sangha, the Buddha arrived at a strategy to overcome every form of asava, which is elliptically outlined in one Buddhist text:

> It is wise if one makes use of medicine and other necessities for the sick if the view is only to ward off the pain that causes injury, and to preserve the sufferer's health.

---

[33] Meng, *et al.*, "The Origins of Cannabis Smoking", pp. 5–6.
[34] *Vinaya Texts*, Mahavagga, VI, 1–40, pp. 41–143.

If one is not using them correctly, asava may arise, causing vexation and distress; whereas to the man making right use, the asavas, full of vexation and distress, are not in evidence.[35]

This strategy to deal with drug addiction by prohibiting certain sorts of food and drink, even while exempting the medicinal benefits of drugs, was the foundation of the Buddhist concept of human health. Inviting physicians to treat illnesses and using herbal ingredients as medicine were acknowledged concepts of medical care based on a history of experience and experimentation. Establishing sanitation guidelines towards building a healthy community within the chaotic environment of early urbanisation distinguished Buddhist personal hygiene and public health from Brahmanical notions of purity and pollution.

In contemporary and later Brahman dharmic literature, physicians who practise medicine to heal people are considered polluting. According to Gautama, food given by a surgeon and other such polluting professionals, such as police officers, must not be eaten.[36] In Vasistha's law, a Brahman who makes a living by practising medicine is not a Brahman any more than a man who lives by trades such as acting, or a common thief.[37] Foods provided by a physician were suspect in the same way as those sold by a soma plant seller or a seller of liquor.[38] It is not as if Brahmans did not consult physicians or refused their medicines; their view of the medicine man was more an attitude of condescension and superiority in relation to people they considered tradesmen and peddlers of drugs. Perhaps plenty of physicians such as Jivaka were also born in humble households and were of low status, and thus seen as polluting. The Buddhist sangha, by contrast, viewed human malady more rationally, seeing the value of physicians who possessed the expertise required in ridding humanity of some of its pain.

[35] *All the Asavas* [*Sabbasava Sutta*], 27–8, p. 304.
[36] Gautama, *Institutes of the Sacred Law*, XVII, 17, p. 267.
[37] *Vasistha Dharmasastra*, III.8, p. 17.
[38] Ibid., XIV, 2, p. 69.

4

Supporters in the Cities

Gahapati, Setthi, Visakha, and Women who Fed the Sangha

WE HAVE SEEN earlier that the gahapati (householder) and the setthi (lit. an "elder") embodied the new social and economic elite active in the development of an agricultural society. Cities arose as hubs of commerce, manufacture, and administration for new territorial states in the shape of kingdoms or ganasanghas. A gahapati was the head of a household, an economic entity with landholdings or a business, and a family of two or three generations plus servants and slaves. Though some gahapatis engaged in trade and others in agriculture, most of them, judging from the descriptions in Pali literature, took residence in the cities from where they conducted their business, leaving the villages to cultivators and artisans. Gahapatis linked the urban and rural economies. Setthis could also be either city dwellers or people living outside the major cities. "Setthi" comes from the Sanskrit word "Shreshthin", the superlative case of "shri", which means "the best" and can also mean "the eldest". Buddhist literature uses both terms together: "Gahapatis and Setthis". Their prestige attached to the title "setthi" was not so much related to their seniority as elders, as to their wealth and role in finance within the emerging monetary system. Setthis were superior to gahapatis in status.

Gahapatis and setthis living in or around major cities such as Rajagaha of Magadha, Savatthi of Kosala, and Vesali of the Vajji Ganasangha were all aware of each others' existence, their families often intermarrying to facilitate and consolidate their businesses. Anathapindika was a rich gahapati in the city of Savatthi who married the sister of a setthi – his business partner in the city of Rajagaha. Anathapindika was also an exemplary gahapati in the Buddhist sangha, for he not only followed the teachings of the Buddha but also donated to it a garden resort called Jetavana near the city of Savatthi, where the Buddha sojourned and gave numerous sermons. Anathapindika, meaning "giver to forlorn people", was not his real name but he was almost exclusively known by it on account of his famed generosity.

It had all started when Anathapindika arrived at the home of his brother-in-law, the setthi of Rajagaha, for business.[1] At this point the setthi was busy organising his household for a big feast and could not even greet Anathapindika in the customary way. Gahapati Anathapindika did manage to learn that the guests for whom the preparations were afoot would be the Buddha and his sangha. The very title "Buddha" – the Enlightened – took the gahapati by surprise and he decided to seek out the famed sage for his own enlightenment the next morning.

Looking for the Buddha was not easy as he dwelt in a woody area called Sitavana, which was out of Anathapindika's comfort zone. He proceeded timorously and finally reached the Buddha only at the urging and encouragement of Sivaka, a Yakkha – Yakkhas being people outside the mainstream of the Sanskrit-Prakrit communities. These were people who spoke different languages and worshipped various cults. This Yakkha, Sivaka, happened to be friendly both with the Buddhist sangha and with Anathapindika who was seeking the Buddha.

Happening to be strolling up and down in Sitavana at dawn,

---

[1] The full story is included in the *Vinaya Texts*, Cullavagga VI.4, 1–10, pp. 179–89.

the Buddha saw Anathapindika and greeted him by calling out his personal name, which was Sudatta. The two immediately struck up a rapport; Anathapindika became a disciple who learned the Buddha's Four Noble Truths. Following their first meeting, Anathapindika hosted the feast for the sangha the next day – the one under preparation in the house of his brother-in-law, the setthi in Rajagaha.

After finishing with his business in Rajagaha, Anathapindika returned to Savatthi. His determination now was to set up a garden resort near his city where the Buddha could come and teach. His experience in seeking and meeting the Buddha at Sitavana may have prompted this resolve to create an accessible resort for the Buddha and his sangha:

> Where now shall I fix the place for the Blessed one to stay in, not too far from the town and not too near, convenient for going and for coming, easily accessible for all who wish to visit him, by day not crowded, by night not exposed to too much noise and alarm, protected from the wind, hidden from men, well fitted for retired life?[2]

This locating of a resort for the Buddha, though not as a permanent residence, was a foretaste of the special role of Buddhist settlements in the region's society. The location needed to be accessible for lay followers from the cities but not be submerged by urban chaos. Though not explicitly stated, such resorts needed also to keep the sangha in contact with the wild terrains where Yakkha, Naga, and other non-conformist communities lived.

Anathapindika's search for such a location took him to a Kosala prince named Jeta, from whom he purchased the garden with – it was said – so many gold coins that they covered nearly the entire enclosure that they were payment for. At Jeta's insistence that a corner not paid for by Anathapindika be reserved as the prince's portion, the garden retained its name and continued to be known as Jetavana.

[2] Ibid., VI.4.8, p. 187.

To make the garden a liveable place, it was said Anathapindika had facilities built within it: "Dwelling-rooms, and retiring-rooms, and store-rooms (over the gateways), and service halls, and halls with fire-places in them, and storehouses (outside the vihara), and closets, and cloisters, and halls for exercise, and wells, and sheds for the well, and bath-rooms, and halls attached to the bath-rooms, and ponds, and open-roofed sheds."[3]

This elaborate building complex could not possibly have been the single-handed creation of Anathapindika at the instance of the Buddhist sangha. This passage, on constructions which may have been carried out by several contributors over the years, reveals the development of the Buddhist sangha as an institution, from its inception as a group of roaming mendicants to a firmer establishment where followers could gather in sheltered locations for learning, meditation, rest, and a sense of discipline. When the sangha created a dress code to signify their difference from other sects, stores were needed for the clothing and vessels used in initiation ceremonies. A well for drawing water and bathrooms were necessary facilities as well for the sangha to maintain personal hygiene and public sanitation. Space for exercise that helped keep Buddhists healthy was yet another requirement. Anathapindika and his possible successors were thus creating what was intended as a template for the shelter and nurture of the Buddha's expanding number of devotees.

Jetavana earned Anathapindika's praise as the first almsgiver of the Buddhist sangha.[4] With Jetavana in the suburbs of Savatthi, Anathapindika could now frequent the garden to hear the Buddha teach and be present at religious services performed by his senior disciples Sariputta and Ananda. Once, it is reported, Anathapindika ventured out of curiosity into a nearby camp of other recluses and there listened to views about the nature of life, the soul, and the universe from philosophers, and he there also voiced his own views based on the teachings of the Buddha. It was said that Anathapindika's eloquence was so great that all the listening philosophers felt

---

[3] Ibid., VI.4.10, p. 189.
[4] *Anguttara-Nikāya*, I.14, §26, p. 23.

lost for words by the time he ended his discourse. Upon hearing his report of the interaction, the Buddha exclaimed to his disciples: "Monks, any monk who had been fully ordained in this dhamma-discipline even for a hundred rain-seasons might reasonably from time to time confute and rebuke Wanderers holding other views just as they have been confuted by the housefather Anathapindika."[5]

Anathapindika was a householder, not a monk. The Buddha and his disciples are believed to have returned his generosity with spiritual and practical services. Once, the Buddha walked into Anathapindika's household and there heard much commotion. Sitting down with the householder, he heard that his daughter-in-law, Sujata, though from a wealthy and respectable family, was overly assertive and had refused to obey her parents-in-law, and gone to the extent of defying even her husband. She had thus created chaos in the household. The Buddha summoned the young woman and said: "Sujata, a man may have these seven kinds of wives. What seven? One like a slayer, one like a robber, one like a mistress, one like a mother, one like a sister, one like a companion, and one like a handmaid. These, Sujata, are the seven; and which of them are you?"[6] When Sujata requested that he expand on these categories, the Buddha provided her with the characteristics of each kind of wife; he then declared that wives with the character of mother, sister, companion, and slave (handmaiden) would ascend to heaven after their death, while those who were mistresses, slayers, and thieves would descend into hell. Sujata thought this over, and though she saw she had four options to secure her position in heaven, she swore nevertheless that she would henceforth fit herself into the humblest category of wife and be a handmaiden.[7] To belong to this category of wife meant enduring all kinds of abuse, such as whippings and thrashings, and yet remain obedient and loyal. It is hard to imagine Sujata the shrew willingly wanting to be reduced to this form of subjecthood, especially as she had three other modestly superior

[5] Ibid., X, X, 93, 185–9, pp. 127–30.
[6] Ibid., VII, VI, 59b, p. 56.
[7] Ibid., p. 58.

options, i.e. to be a mother, sister, or companion, either of which would still have kept her out of hell. Perhaps within a business family, the ideal wife was in fact the handmaiden and Sujata was only expressing what was expected of her. The household she had come into was not merely a family but a business entity structured along a functional hierarchy. This would have been a business ladder with the patriarch as its pivot, and it could not afford to be disturbed by the tantrums and wilfulness of a daughter-in-law, regardless of the higher status of her natal family. *Plus ça change, plus c'est la même chose*. The Buddha's admonition restored the order necessary to the functional home of Anathapindika the householder.

The day dawned when Anathapindika knew that despite his understanding of the Four Noble Truths of the Buddha, he needed the consolation of the sangha at the crucial moment of his death: he was seriously ill and dying. The Buddha and his senior disciples, who often stayed in Jetavana, cared for Anathapindika at this time. Sariputta treated his bedsores and assured him recovery from the pain; hours of talk comforted the householder; for a time he felt better and had a meal from his own cooking pot served to Sariputta, who reported progress to the Buddha and received his praise.[8]

Sometime later Anathapindika fell really sick and again asked Sariputta to his bedside. Sensing the severity of the situation, both Sariputta and Ananda went to the householder who was leaving the world in great pain and agony. To him Sariputta and Ananda said:

> Wherefore you, householder, must train yourself thus: [you must think] "I will not grasp after vision and so will have no consciousness dependent on vision." This is how you must train yourself, householder. Wherefore you, householder, must train yourself thus: [You must think] I will not grasp after hearing . . . smelling . . . tasting . . . body . . . mind . . . material shapes . . . sounds . . . smells . . . tastes . . . touches . . . mental objects and so will have no consciousness dependent on mental objects.[9]

[8] *Sanyutta-Nikaya*, pt V, LV, XI, III, vi, pp. 329–32.
[9] *Majjhima-Nikaya*, III.259, p. 310.

The final service over, Anathapindika rose to the heavens of the devas, the highest place in the realm of life cycles before nirvana.[10] He thus became a young deva who would enjoy a pleasant existence in heaven, though even there he would continue needing to accrue merit lest he fall back into the human world or even lower. Helping their greatest patron to leave the world with peace of mind was the best reward the Buddhist sangha offered its disciples.

Many women supported the early sangha over the lifetime of the Buddha even though they were not part of the bhikkhuni sangha. In Buddhist literature, women feature not just as wives and mothers but also as active individual agents engaged in their own pursuits. Their existence in urban life was a matter of fact, but these extra-familial roles did not fit with Brahmanical moral models and social regulations of convention. Seeking guidance from the Buddha on what was correct and ethical in social interaction, rather than blind adherence to Brahmanical stricture, made sense to such people. Some of them, such as Visakha, were engaged in business within the urban economy and lived an affluent life. Giving alms to the sangha meant she could get advice from the Buddha when in distress and ensure a good afterlife for herself in the great scheme of rebirth. In turn, promising a good afterlife to disciples secured for the sangha a daily supply of meals and an annual supply of clothing for its personnel, even as this reciprocal arrangement served as a beacon for potential lay followers to join the order. The Buddha himself took great pains to explain that present sufferings were the consequences of meritorious or wicked deeds in former lives, which served to caution his following on the constant need for virtue in daily life.

With the expansion of the sangha, its dependence on the good will of lay followers to feed and clothe them became ever more imperative. Once the Buddha had passed away it became even more important for his chief disciples to elaborate on his rebirth scheme: their lay patrons had to stay convinced that meals and clothes given to the sangha really did move those who were generous in their

---

[10] Ibid., III.261–2, pp. 313–14.

donations towards happier afterlives. The argument to be made convincingly to the laity was that feeding and clothing monks and nuns was the foremost merit-generating act.

Women were the primary audience the sangha had to address in this matter, for it was the women who cooked the meals and served the sangha. Many of the women who prepared the victuals served the food themselves as well, whereas men who made the donations had their wives or women servants cook and serve the meals to the bhikkhus and bhikkhunis. These women, rich or poor, stayed outside the sangha and served the sangha, but they neither joined the sangha while alive nor were deemed fit to enter the state of nirvana ("nibbana" in Pali) when dying. It would seem that in the aftermath of the Buddha's passing, a group of Pali texts in a category called *Khuddaka-nikaya* (Minor Texts) were used by monks and nuns to promote patronage by lay society. In one of these *Khuddaka-nikaya* works, the major disciple Maha-Moggallana initiated the elaboration of stories of the afterlives of lay women patrons into a text called *Vimanavatthu* – Stories of the Mansions.

When thinking about lay followers, men and women, who were not of sufficient merit to attain the final bliss, Moggallana suggested that they had ascended to a celestial place. He surmised that this elevation put them where the devas, the gods of the Vedic tradition, lived. Moggallana then decided to make a personal tour of this deva world to investigate the nature of good deeds the people there had done when alive – the meritorious acts that had enabled them to ascend to the heavens. His purpose in making such a tour was to bring their life stories back into the earthly world as examples for the edification of lay followers.[11] In the heavenly world of Sakka, the Buddhist name for the Vedic god Indra, there were apparently many splendid mansions filled with resident lay followers of the Buddha. The Buddhists called this territory of heavenly mansions the Heaven of Thirty-three – the court of Sakka, king of the gods.[12]

---

[11] *Vimanavatthu*, IV.X.xvii.

[12] The Tāvatiṃsa (Pali) or Trāyastriṃśa (Sanskrit) heaven in Buddhist cosmology was thought to belong to thirty-three devas.

And it seems that most residents of the mansions in the Heaven of Thirty-three were women, they being those who had performed most of the services to the sangha while on earth. Some of these women – those among them who deserved something even greater than a life serving Sakka – ascended to an even higher heaven where the devas themselves lived and married the women who had been elevated as high up as the devas themselves.

Visakha was one such woman who had entered the world of the gods. According to anecdotes in the *Vinaya* and other early Pali texts, she was a rich matriarch who lived in Savatthi. Everyone knew her as "Mother of Migara", her husband and natal family appearing only in a later commentary of the *Dhammapada*. The reconstructed story says that she was born in a big setthi household in the city of Bhaddiya in Magadha state. At age sixteen, she heard a sermon by the Buddha in her native city. After her family moved to the territory of Kosala, she was married to a setthi of Savatthi and thus entered the household of an unbeliever. She managed to convert her parents-in-law to serve the Buddhist sangha – perhaps by making them fear the prospect of hell after their deaths – but she failed to similarly convince her husband to join the faith.[13] However, it seems Visakha held the purse strings and ran the business of the household she was married into. In Buddhist literature, her own name and motherhood are thus her identity. The Buddha and his sangha often sojourned in her storeyed mansion and her considerable business involved the Kosala royal family. She was once so distressed when a business negotiation with King Pasenadi failed that she rushed to the Buddha – who happened to be in her house – even though it was a bad time of day, to bemoan her loss. The Buddha consoled her and relieved her of the pain of a failed business deal.[14]

Another instance narrates the Buddha staying in her house at the time when her beloved granddaughter died. Once again she

---

[13] Horner, in *Women under Primitive Buddhism*, has reconstructed Visakha's life story: idem, pp. 345–61.

[14] *Udana* II, ix, II, pp. 22–3.

rushed to the Buddha – again at an inopportune hour – to seek his consolation.[15] The death of a loved one was the best occasion for the Buddhist teaching of detachment, and to have the Buddha himself at hand over a time of grief was the most precious consolation possible.

That the Buddha seems to have been around for her so frequently was to some extent due to the fact that she was one of the greatest patrons of his sangha. Visakha made numerous donations to the sangha during his lifetime, especially during the process of the establishment of a dress code and a healthy environment for bhikkhus and bhikkhunis. Once, in heavy rain, she prepared a meal for the Buddha and his followers, but they were unable to partake of it on account of being drenched. They were able to avail of her hospitality the following day, which was when she asked permission from the Buddha to donate to the sangha: "I desire, Lord, my life long to bestow robes for the rainy season on the sangha, and food for in-coming Bhikkhus, and food for out-going Bhikkhus, and food for the sick and food for those [who] wait upon the sick, and medicine for the sick, and a constant supply of congey [rice milk], and bathing robes for the nuns."[16] The Buddha then asked her why she wanted to do all this, and why in particular bathing robes for bhikkhunis. Visakha had this to say on the matter:

> Now, Lord, the bhikkhunis are in the habit of bathing in the river Aciravati with the courtesans, at the same landing-place, and naked. And the courtesans, Lord, ridiculed the bhikkhunis, saying, "What is the good, ladies, of your maintaining chastity when young? Are not the passions things to be indulged? When you are old, maintain chastity then; thus will you be obtainers of both ends." Then the bhikkhunis, Lord, when thus ridiculed by the courtesans, were confused. Impure, Lord, is nakedness for a woman, disgusting, and revolting. It was this circumstance, Lord, that I had in view in desiring to provide the bhikkhuni-sangha my life long with dresses to bathe in.[17]

---

[15] Ibid., VIII, viii, pp. 111–12.
[16] *Vinaya Texts*, Mahavagga 15, pp. 216–25, quotation on pp. 219–20.
[17] Ibid., pp. 222–3.

The safety of women in the sangha was clearly a concern that Visakha was voicing. Not only should they be robed, as were the bhikkhus, they also needed covering when bathing alongside other women, such as entertainers and the sex workers of the city. It seems there were no secluded bathing places for bhikkhunis; specially designed bathing robes would mark their status off from other women living outside households. In other words, even if the bhikkhuni sangha seemed to be an established institution, women's vulnerability to harassment and extreme weather remained unresolved issues.

In the city of Vesali, Ambapali donated her mansion to the sangha – this was where Maha Pajapati and other elder sisters later lived. In the city of Savatthi, Queen Mallika's garden hosted bhikkhunis, even if the house was not meant exclusively for them, but then even the famous Jetavana given to the sangha by Anathapindika was more a garden with some shelter than a permanent residence. Visakha too wanted to donate a house to the sangha, in particular to the bhikkhuni sangha. She pleaded with the Buddha to have a storeyed mansion (*pasada*), with a verandah (*alinda*) built for the sangha, and the Buddha indicated agreement with his silence.[18] However, there is no record that she actually had such a house built.

There are other versions of Visakha's desire to donate a house to the bhikkhunis. One story goes that her opportunity came when she attended a sermon of the Buddha in her city. She is depicted as an opulent lady wearing a legendary "great creeper parure" of precious jewels and surrounded by hundreds of female servants when travelling. Once, when she was in the Buddha's presence, Visakha decided she should take off her jewellery as a sign of respect for the great mendicant. The slave girl who was entrusted with holding her jewellery forgot the treasure and left it in the sangha. Having learned that her parure had been left in the sangha, Visakha made it a donation to be used for a magnificent building for the use of the sangha. The worth of the jewellery proved far more substantial than the cost of building the mansion, the construction of which was supervised

---

[18] Cullavagga, VI.14.1, in *Vinaya Texts*, pt III, p. 130.

by Maha-Moggallana. Once the construction was over, Visakha performed its dedication ceremony with a large female retinue and declared to the assembled women: "Whatever merit I have gained in building a palace such as this, do you rejoice in it; I confer upon you merits therein for participation."[19]

Yet another story narrates Visakha having a vihara built for the sangha, but not necessarily for the bhikkhuni sangha. Her intention in making the donation, she declared, was that the merit acquired therefrom be shared by her women companions. In this narration, hers was a wish for a residence for the bhikkhuni sangha that she suspected might not be realised in this world, so she wanted it to happen in the next world. A mansion for women thus appeared in the Heaven of Thirty-three, and the women who had shared in Visakha's earthly merit entered this women's vihara of the celestial Sakka world. Meanwhile, Visakha herself had acquired so much merit that this heaven was not exalted enough for her status after her exit from the world of the living. She was meant for another, even more beautiful and joyful heaven where music played incessantly; this heaven was the Sumimmita heaven, and here she was the chief consort of the king of the devas.[20]

In sum, what we can infer from the stories about Visakha is that "heaven" for her was an impulse towards idealism which took the shape of her dream for a happy dwelling place for Buddhist sisters. She may not have been able to bring about its existence within her own lifetime, which made her project it all the more as something that would be realised in her afterlife. She was also, it seems clear, a generous patron who never joined the sangha herself. Her husband is never really around, and she is mainly the embodiment of female power: she is the powerful matriarch, the loving mother and grandmother, and her central concern is to protect the bhikkhunis of the sangha. It is very possible that Visakha's independence, chastity, and generosity bothered cultures of patriarchal power in subsequent periods – this may underlie the desire in Buddhist writers

---

[19] *Vimanavatthu*, 6 *Viharavimana*, pp. 86–90.
[29] Ibid., p. 88.

soon after the lifetime of the Buddha to show her with a husband, albeit a divine one in a very high heaven.

Another great patron of the Buddhist sangha was Uttara, and she too is known from the time of the Buddha. She was known by her son's name – Mother of Nanda – rather than her husband's because he was not a Buddhist. In early Pali texts she appears in a list as one of the best female lay followers of the Buddha.[21] In *Vimanavatthu* her father Punna is a hired labourer cultivating land for a setthi of Rajagaha. When the time of a festival approaches, the setthi asks Punna whether he wants to go off to the festival or continue working and earn more money. Punna, being too poor to enjoy the festivity, chooses to continue ploughing his master's fields.

Now it so happened that Sariputta, the Buddhist elder, decided to rest himself in a bush at the edge of the field. Out of devotion upon seeing him, Punna made a toothbrush from a twig, and along with water that he carried to work, served the elder. Then, when Punna's wife was carrying cooked rice to her husband, she saw Sariputta and offered all of it to him. After this virtuous offering, the woman hurried home to cook more rice for her husband. Finishing his meal late, Punna was tired and fell asleep. When he awoke, he saw the field in front was covered with gold. Punna was rich! In view of all his new-found gold, the king of Rajagaha made him a setthi, and thus he joined the urban elite. Punna's former boss then saw fit to ask for the hand of Uttara, daughter of Punna, for his son. Uttara was reluctant to marry into this family because they were unbelievers. Social pressure in the city eventually forced Punna to give in, for the nouveau riche could hardly refuse an alliance offer from established old money.

The miracle of dirt transformed to gold could suggest a time when farming was profitable and even a labouring peasant could aspire to be a setthi. The plausible alternative is of course the provisioning of a hallowed genealogy for Uttara by subsequent Buddhist hagiographical and devotional literature.

Uttara was unhappy in her marital home because she was not

[21] *Anguttara-Nikāya*, text 1.26, p. 24; ibid., text iv, pp. 345, 229.

allowed to feed Buddhist monks. By the time the rainy season of that year drew to an end and the great festival of feeding the sangha approached, she was so desperate that she sent a plaintive message to her father. Punna then came up with a strategy for Uttara to get permission from her husband to feed the sangha. He sent 15,000 gold coins to his daughter to hire the most beautiful courtesan in town, Sirima, to serve her husband for fifteen days. This would allow Uttara freedom to cook for the sangha. Captivated by Sirima, Uttara's husband readily agreed to the deal and allowed Uttara to spend all fifteen festival days cooking for the sangha.[22]

It seems that Uttara never managed to convert her husband to Buddhism, and so was to the end called "Mother of Nanda" by the Buddhists. After her death, she ascended to the Heaven of Thirty-three and resided in her own mansion as a beautiful devata or demi-goddess.

Sirima, in her turn, also became a faithful follower of the Buddha. Her service to the sangha and obeisance to the teaching of the Buddha helped her as well as other women from the margins of mainstream society into the fold of Buddhist followers. In their cosmic hierarchy they progressed from the edge of the earth to heaven. Sirima was, as remarked, the most beautiful and famous courtesan in Rajagaha. She was the youngest daughter of the courtesan Salavati, who had given birth to Jivaka the physician and abandoned him.[23] There is no record of the origins of Salavati, except that she was beautiful and established by Bimbisara himself as *the* courtesan of Rajagaha to draw in business. She never enjoyed the same prestige as Ambapali, who represented the city of Vesali, but she was well known all the same. Sirima was, like Salavati, from a matrilineal courtesan family of the kind that cast out their male infants but groomed their girls for the profession. So when Sirima came of age she duly followed in her mother's footsteps and became a famous

[22] *Vimanavatthu*, 15 *Uttaravimana*, IV, pp. 24–8.
[23] For the story of Salavati and Jivaka, see *Vinaya Texts*, Mahavagga, viii.1, pp. 171ff.; for the story of Sirima, see *Vimanavatthu*, 16 *Sirimāvimāna*, pp. 32–7.

courtesan, well trained in dance and song, and able to charge customers huge sums for a full night's work.[24] Sirima died young and suddenly from unknown causes, a quite common phenomenon among residents of these early insanitary cities, even more among those in her profession. Courtesans entertained and mingled with both city residents and travellers from other places, and tended to use stimulants for performance enhancement, which made them vulnerable to contagious diseases. Had it not been for her encounter with Uttara in the household of the setthi, Sirima would not have been known to later Buddhists.

The story of her time as replacement wife is detailed. When substituting for Uttara in the performance of duties as the setthi's wife, Sirima fell in love with her new status as mistress in a rich household and thus forgot she was there only temporarily. Meanwhile the setthi was amused by how engrossed Uttara was in cooking and serving food to bhikkhus and bhikkhunis. He smiled at her in the kitchen and said she was silly to be giving up a life of leisure. This made Sirima jealous, for she had come to believe the setthi was her own husband. She took hold of a ladle in the kitchen and, scooping hot oil into it, poured its contents on Uttara's head. Miraculously, Uttara was not hurt, the story goes, in part as she recalled that Sirima was doing her a great service by letting her gain merit through service to the sangha, and by remembering also that tolerance of ill intent would fetch her even more merit. However, various maidservants who were also busy in the kitchen, discerning their real mistress in harm's way, thronged against Sirima to counter her attack. Uttara had to step in and separate her servants from Sirima. A surprised Sirima was now predisposed by Uttara's act of benevolence to the teaching of the Buddha, in which direction Uttara was happy to guide her.[25]

Sirima now became a pious devotee of the Buddha, serving meals for eight members of the sangha every day. Her stunning beauty,

---

[24] *Vimanavatthu*, 15 *Uttaravimana*, IV, pp. 24–32.
[25] Ibid.

unfortunately, caught the eye of bhikkhus who had not sufficiently quelled their earthly passions, one of whom was so stricken with lovesickness for her that he took to his bed and stopped eating and drinking. The very night that the besotted monk beheld her and began to pine for her, the story goes, was the night that Sirima perished. Hearing of her death, the Buddha took the opportunity to teach the fallen bhikkhu as well as the general public a lesson on the impermanence of physical beauty. He sent a message to the king advising that Sirima's body be laid in the funeral grounds to decompose for three days. He then summoned bhikkhus, bhikkhunis, and all the king's men and his lay followers to behold her rotting corpse and bade the king auction her body for 1000 gold coins – her price for one night in her company when alive – then for 500, then for 250, all the way down to zero. There being no takers at such an auction, the disconsolate bhikkhu forsook all passion and understood most truly the illusory nature of physical beauty. Meanwhile, Sirima had long left the shell of her body and been reshaped as a celestial beauty who dwelt in one of the mansions of the Heaven of Thirty-three by virtue of having served the sangha.[26]

Despite never having had the good fortune of membership of the sangha, Sirima came to be embedded in the collective memory of Buddhists for centuries to come. On the railings of the Bharhut Stupa, dated to the second century BCE, an exquisitely executed human-sized statue of Sirima Devata was set up to convince later women followers that she, a woman from the margins, had achieved what many others had not, quite simply by feeding the Buddhist sangha (Fig. 6).

Visakha, Uttara, and Sirima were influential women in cities during the time of the Buddha. Yet memories of their lives have been preserved only in Buddhist literature. No matter how rich and famous they were within their societies, they had no role to play in Brahmanical rituals and therefore there are no records of their existence. Visakha could not seek the advice of a Brahman for her

[26] *Vimanavatthu*, 16 *Sirimāvimana*, pp. 32–7.

Fig. 6: Sirima Devata, Bharhut Stupa, Indian Museum catalogue 141, American Institute of Indian Studies, photo negative no. 23.71, courtesy of the Library of the University of Pennsylvania.

business problems; Sirima relied on her faith in the teachings of the Buddha to face death and the afterlife. Their supply of provisions to the sangha, which helped the survival and development of the sangha, also set them up as role models for lay patrons in literature and artworks, and this has preserved their stories.

In addition to the rich and famous, many women who served the sangha with donations and food were assured mansions in heaven. A special mansion for a slave woman, a dasivimana, was positioned in a heaven meant for women who had provided meals to bhikkhus. One particular slave woman cooked food for the sangha on behalf of her master, became an attendant of a Sakka, and had some 6000 musicians and dancers under her command.[27] No personal name is recorded in the text, probably because she was merely female and a slave. But some of the heavenly musicians and dancers were well known in Buddhist literature and art. In a relief panel on the railing of the Bharhut Stupa which displays a celebration of the Buddha's enlightenment in the heavens, four heavenly dancers – accharas in Pali and apsaras in Sanskrit – had names, and three of

Fig. 7: Orchestra and dancing in the heavens, Indian Museum catalogue 273, American Institute of Indian Studies, photo negative no. 484.58, courtesy of the Library of the University of Pennsylvania.

[27] *Vimanavatthu, Cittalatā*, 1, *Dāsīvimāna*, pp. 41–3.

these names – Subhadda, Alambusa, and Missakesi – are part of the list of the "Slave Woman's" entourage (Fig. 7). The Bharhut Stupa was one of the earliest built in India. Artworks on its railings reflect the universe in the minds of Buddhists in the early centuries after the Buddha's death and it became the prototype for Buddhist artists in the ensuing centuries.

In stories about the garden of the Sakka heaven, serving meals to the sangha as an enabling strategy for access to a heavenly mansion is the main theme. Serving the Buddha himself was of course the best guarantee of high merit, and serving great disciples such as Moggallana and Sariputta was nearly as good. Even just feeding monks along a schedule was meritorious. In one story a physician's wife serves a special rice gruel with jujube juice to Ananda when he comes to her door holding the Buddha's own bowl. The woman recognises the bowl and sees that Ananda has brought it because the Buddha is unwell. Further, as the wife of a physician who has imbibed some medical knowledge, she discerns that the Buddha's stomach is the problem and that he needs nutritious soft food.[28] Buddhists remember her with affection on account of her tale in *Vimanavatthu*.

The stories also reveal a pattern in the assigning of merit to women who fed the sangha. In the earliest days of the sangha the Buddha himself, together with a group of followers, roamed from city to city, being fed by rich gahapatis and setthis. With the expansion of the sangha, bhikkhus and bhikkhunis began spreading out on their own to preach the dhamma, each with an individual bowl. They would sojourn either at resting places such as Jetavana, which was designated for the sangha, or else take shelter in caves along hills adjoining their path. Even in the larger cities, feeding the entire wandering community of Buddhists became quite a big operation and required substantial outlays by affluent patrons. Simultaneously, less affluent lay devotees seem to have shouldered the burden of

---

[28] *Vimanavatthu*, III, *Paricchattaka, Kanjikadayka, Gruel giver's Mansion*, pp. 85–6.

feeding individual brothers and sisters along a fixed schedule. Providing meals for eight monks every day, as Sirima did, became the standard method if the devotee wanted to acquire the higher credit of feeding a group within the sangha as a group, and not just stray individuals. Those who could afford to feed eight monks signed up to do so and thereby gained more points in the snakes-and-ladders game of up towards heaven or down towards endless rebirths.

In one story narrated on the theme of feeding groups of eight, a woman named Bhadda, married into a rich family, is barren. She persuades her husband to marry her sister, Subhadda, to replenish the family. Both sisters belong to a devoted family serving a Buddhist elder called Revata. Bhadda advises her sister to continue serving this elder when she enters her new household. Subhadda consents and invites seven more brother monks when feeding the elder Revata, and thus reaches the minimum required for higher merit in her heavenly account. After her death Bhadda reaches the Heaven of Thirty-three while Subhadda ascends to an even higher position and joins the company of the devas. In her celestial world Subhadda remembers the good advice given to her by her sister and wanders around to look for Bhadda, who meanwhile is puzzled by her inferior status in heaven since she was the one who initiated the meritorious action. She now comes to understand that serving eight members of the sangha means more merit in one's future lives and learns a valuable lesson that she can carry over to make matters better for herself when reborn.[29]

Bhadda and Subhadda are common names in the Buddhist Pali texts, but the story of these two sisters sharing a husband is no doubt intended to set up a merit hierarchy showing what constitutes best practice even within a single family. Feeding eight monks elevates Subhadda one ladder above her sister: the moral of the story is obvious. It is worth recalling here that Sirima only reaches the lower regions of the Sakka heaven despite serving the required

---

[29] *Vimanavatthu*, III, *Paricchattaka, Daddalhvimana*, pp. 67–71.

eight. Why is she not placed higher? The answer may lie in the fact that she had a lower start on account of her poor initial status and questionable morals before she was converted to the right path.

Various other women in disadvantaged situations are shown to reach the Sakka heavens if they really make the required effort to gather merit. A woman named Lakhuma from the Fisherman's Gate of the city of Baranasi (Benares) was apparently from a fishing community. Being involved in the meat business, she will have been from a very low caste, or of no caste in the Brahmanical hierarchy. She nevertheless earned merit by devotedly serving food to monks, and by having a pavilion built as a refuge for wandering bhikkhus and bhikkhunis.[30] The Sakka heavens also contained three daughters-in-law killed by their mothers-in-law for feeding monks without permission.[31]

The beneficence of the Buddha and his sangha is also shown in stories where they do not ignore the sufferings of women who are so miserably placed that they lack all means to serve the sangha. To such women the Buddha's guidance was to retain a vision of aspiring to the heavens even if they were unable to make virtuous donations in their current lives.

Outside the cities there lived communities of outcastes who performed the most polluting yet essential work of cleaning and tending cremation grounds. These people, called Candalas (Chandalas) and Candalis (Chandalis), lacked all respect in villages and cities. The Buddha sympathised with these outcastes but was not able to do much for their material improvement. In *Vimanavatthu* a feeble elderly woman, a Candali, encounters the Buddha outside the city of Rajagaha and honours him by crouching in the most craven and therefore the most perfect posture of respect. She is shown as having ascended to the Sakka heavens, where she resides in a mansion reserved for Candalis.[32] Reserving a mansion in the heaven for Candalis suggests that Buddhists respected those

[30] *Vimanavatthu, Cittalatā*, 1, *Lakhumavimana*, pp. 43–5.
[31] *Vimanavatthu,* 1 (29), pp. 57–8; 2 (30), pp. 59–61; 10 (48), p. 96.
[32] *Vimanavatthu, Cittalatā*, 1, *Candalivimana*, pp. 47–9.

of lowest status. For the Candala community, merely to have the respect of the Buddha and his sangha was sufficient encouragement to follow the teachings of the Buddha, and thus to improve their chances of being reborn into a better existence.

Then there are the women who have been wronged by society. One such is Rajjumala, a slave girl in a Brahman household in Gaya – the location of the Buddha's enlightenment. Her mistress, who is the daughter-in-law of the household, is so awful that she often drags Rajjumala around by her hair. Rajjumala has her hair cut, which makes her mistress even angrier; she ties Rajjumala with a cord around her neck and drags her around by it and calls her "Rajjumala the cord-wreathed" to torture her. One evening when Rajjumala is sent to fetch water, she is ready to hang herself on a tree. At that very moment the Buddha comes across her and instructs her on the Four Noble Truths. Rajjumala gains her composure and returns with a new spring in her step, surprising the householder, whom she proceeds to convince that further torture of her could be bad for the household. Thereupon her mistress desists and matters improve. Rajjumala eventually ascends to the mansion of Rajjumalavimanla in the Sakka heavens.[33] Her story is the Buddhist allegorical way of saying that material deprivation resulting in an inability to assist the sangha matters less than heeding the words of the Buddha and becoming a believer. The story of Rajjumala, which is reported as happening around Gaya, also works as testimony that the sage's First Noble Truth – that life is full of suffering – was based on his actual observation and experiences of the living poor.

The scheme of rebirth was much less forgiving with women who deliberately obstructed almsgiving and were hostile to monks. Revativimana, a mansion in the Sakka heavens, lies empty because the resident for whom it was designated, Revati, was the mean-spirited wife of a great patron. Her husband Nandiya built a vihara

---

[33] *Vimanavatthu, IV Manjetthaka (Crimson),* 12 *Rajjumalāvimala,* pp. 97–101.

for the sangha and served the sangha good meals. His wife Revati, who was in charge of cooking and serving, should therefore have been in a heavenly mansion alongside her husband. But she had been a reluctant server of food to the sangha. Any time her husband was absent or not supervising, she served bad meals and mixed fish and meat in them, thus depriving the monks of merit that would otherwise have been theirs. Nandiya discovered this and had her sent back to her own home, though he continued to provide her sustenance, gaining merit for himself thereby. The Buddhists who compiled *Vimanavatthu* had no sympathy for this abandoned wife Revati, consigning her to the most hideous purgatory and leaving her mansion in the heavens conspicuously empty as a warning to women.[34] Neither Nandiya nor Revati were known in early Pali texts.[35] They seem to have been introduced later as warnings to those who failed to provide adequate or proper sustenance to the sangha.

---

[34] *Vimanavatthu*, V., *Maharatha*, 52 *Revatīvimana*, pp. 103–7.
[35] Nandiya as a great patron was referred to in Buddhaghosha's commentary on the *Dhammapada*, III, 219–20, in *The Dhammapada*, p. 185.

5

Bimbisara, Pasenadi, Ajatasattu, and the Vajji Rajas

THE BUDDHIST PALI literature refers to sixteen mahajanapadas (great states) covering the North Indian plains; the Buddha was active not in all sixteen but only in those around the middle and lower Ganges area. Most stories of his activities are in relation to the kingdom of Magadha on the lower Ganges (adjacent to the eastern edge of the Deccan Plateau); in Kosala which covered the territory where Rama of the legends had ruled over his kingdom in antiquity; and in the Vajji Ganasangha Confederation centred in Vesali. The Sakya Ganasangha, where Sakyamuni was born, was a small state perched in the Himalayan foothills which nevertheless played a significant role in the politics of vying for hegemony among the large polities along the plains. In Magadha and Kosala, the two large monarchical states on the eastern Ganges, the rulers came from obscure family lineages and were trying to build a system of succession based on patriarchal primogeniture.

Though the Rama story of the Brahmanical tradition had developed the theme of the righteousness of Ksatriya patriarchal primogeniture and delivered victory to Rama – the eldest son of King Dasaratha of Ayodhya – the story ends without showing a continuation of the rule of Rama's lineage over Kosala. Meanwhile, the "rajas" of the Vajji Ganasangha and the tiny Sakya Ganasangha both claimed Ksatriyahood and were very concerned with maintaining the blood purity of the ruling lineage, which meant a prohibition on elites marrying beyond strictly defined boundaries. In fact warfare, marriage alliances, and the patronage of religious sects all evolved in order to cement boundaries conducive to the institution and perpetuation of a royal household's control of the state. Eventually, the Maurya family of Magadha gained supremacy and conquered all the contiguous major states. Under the third king of the Mauryan dynasty, Ashoka, the empire embraced most parts of South Asia, maintaining the family regime's hold over state power via patriarchal primogeniture in theory, and thus establishing a model of monarchy across much of India.

Senya Bimbisara, king of Magadha, was an earnest supporter of the Buddha. He reigned over a powerful kingdom in his capital city, Rajagaha, which was located in a valley surrounded by mountain peaks. The peaks allowed two passes to link the valley with the Ganges to their north and the Deccan to their south. These natural fortifications made Rajagaha strategically safe for the king, while hill caves around the city provided shelter to various reclusive communities – including that of the Buddha. This was also where, as we have seen, Jivaka, Salavati, and Sirima made their professional medical and cultural mark. Wealth and culture flowed into Rajagaha. News of the glory of the Magadhan kingdom spread far and wide; people of the time admired Bimbisara and believed he was the happiest man in the world.[1]

Like all monarchs of his time, Bimbisara had married strategically to ease rivalries and fend off foes. His wife was a princess from the Kosala kingdom, a sister of Pasenadi, his counterpart in Kosala. From this marriage came Ajatasattu, the crown prince of Magadha.

Bimbisara also married another woman, Khema, a beauty from his own kingdom. At some point he decided to send Khema to the Buddha, who, at the time, was at Venavana, the bamboo garden given to the sangha by the king. The reason, as provided by the commentary in Khema's psalm – which she composed as a senior bhikkhuni later in her life – was her great beauty, which had made her

[1] *Majjhima Nikāya*, I.94, pp. 123–4.

a consort of the king. Apparently Khema was so beautiful that she could not "contain herself", and so the king sent her off to the Buddha where she might learn about the impermanent nature of physical beauty.[2] This excuse for making her depart was probably invented by later commentators since it is incommensurate with the reality of court politics involving marriages within royal households. If Khema was vain and arrogant, the Buddha's reform of her character would logically have entailed her return to the king. But this did not happen. In her psalm, Khema does not mention having children. She was probably married to the king before the arrival of the Kosala princess; her "failure" to produce a child, or a male heir, for Bimbisara may well have been the reason for her exile. To consolidate the position of the Kosala princess and make sure Ajatasattu succeeded him, it would have been a requirement for Bimbisara to displace Khema, and where better than under the custodianship of the Buddha? It seems thus that the Buddha may have been doing the king a favour to ensure a smooth succession. Khema, meanwhile, grew into one of the outstanding disciples of the Buddha. She is even said to have engaged in a theological debate with Kosala's king Pasenadi.[3]

Banishing Khema from the royal household might not have been enough to guarantee Ajatasattu's succession, there being other princes in the household. Abhaya, who raised Jivaka and then recruited him to serve the royal family, would have been a prince senior to Ajatasattu. There is no information on Abhaya's mother or how he was related to Bimbisara, but he was certainly a male contender within the royal family. Another son of Bimbisara, Jayasena, had dialogues with disciples of the Buddha but did not succeed Bimbisara.[4] It was, in sum, a complicated royal household within which succession could be a contentious issue.

Bimbisara first heard of the wisdom of the Buddha when the sage was sojourning in Latthivana, a bamboo grove near Rajagaha, with his bhikkhus. Bimbisara was aware of there being many

[2] Commentary on Khema's psalm, *Therīgāthā*, pp. 81–2.
[3] *Sanyutta Nikāya*, IV, p. 266.
[4] *Majjhima Nikāya*, III, 125, pp. 175ff, 183ff.

Samanas (Sramanas) and Brahmanas in his territory, with Brahmanas being the authority on matters spiritual. The Buddha, though brilliant, was one of the Samanas whose enlightenment, in Uruvela village (later called Gaya), had been within Magadha, not far from Rajagaha. Thus the first choice of location for the Buddha to disseminate his illumination and gain state support was naturally the city of Rajagaha. Bimbisara, with himself at its head, assembled a whole troop of Magadha Brahmanas and householders – i.e. administrative staff, religious advisers, and financial and economic supporters of his regime – to visit the Buddha and discover the nature of his brilliance. The Brahmanas were surprised to find a famous ascetic, Samana Kassapa, in the company of the Buddha and wondered who of the two was the teacher and who the pupil.[5] Kassapa was a fellow ascetic of the Buddha in Uruvela village, where many liberation seekers practised different styles of asceticism. Over a long conversation on the various formats of asceticism and true wisdom, the Buddha had convinced Kassapa that the extreme form of austere asceticism was not the path leading to enlightenment.[6] Now, in front of the king and the Brahmanas, Kassapa declared that he had become a disciple of the Buddha. Bimbisara thereupon decided that the Buddha was the superlative Samana and invited him and his followers to his palace for a feast.[7]

The Buddha and his sangha, over their travels in the Rajagaha region, normally took shelter in caves known as Gridhrakuta (Vulture's Peak), a mountainous area not far from the city. In order to keep the teacher longer and make his visits more frequent, the Magadha king now set up lodgings at Venavana – this being one of the king's own resorts – for the sangha.[8] With the permission of the Buddha, he also had a residence built within the garden precincts.[9] It thus seems that in addition to Jetavana, given by the gahapati Anthapindika near Savatthi, and the mango grove of Jivaka near

---

[5] *Vinaya Texts*, Mahavagga I, 22, 1–3, pp. 136–7.
[6] *Dīgha Nikāya*, vol. I, VIII, *Kassapa-Sīhanāda Sutta*, 161–77, pp. 223–40.
[7] *Vinaya Texts*, Mahavagga I, 22, 15, pp. 142–3.
[8] Ibid., 22, 16–18, p. 143.
[9] Ibid., pt III, Cullavagga, VI, 3, 11, pp. 178–9.

Rajagaha, the Buddha and his sangha had in their early days at least three shelters in three quiet enclosures where they could practise their disciplines and discuss their thoughts. These garden habitats made Buddhists more accessible and closer to the cities; they were convenient enough for monks to walk to urban areas for alms, and conversely for the king and those who wanted to learn from the Buddha to visit them in the outskirts.

These designated resorts for the Buddha and his disciples also made the sangha progressively more like an established institution. The Buddha himself does not seem to have stayed in the Rajagaha region all the time, but, as the sangha expanded, quite a number of bhikkhus took shelter in these vanas. Inevitably, certain deviants and morally dubious elements within society joined the sangha as an escape strategy, and some of the ordained monks did not find favour in the communities around them. This is apparent from the fact that from time to time Bimbisara, as the major royal patron of the sangha in Magadha, had to make a judgement on issues that arose between the monks and the population and then consult the Buddha to solve such problems. In general, the king was generous to the sangha. He opened his mango garden to monks for them to pick mangoes, even though the monks exceeded the spirit of his offer and the king found to his chagrin that no fruit was left for him when he desired some. Even so, Bimbisara was apparently good-natured about it all, saying that the disappearance of the mangoes had served a good purpose.[10]

A more serious issue arose when soldiers at the frontier deserted the army and joined the sangha. This weakening of military force was no laughing matter as it represented a weakening of state power. Bimbisara's conversation with the Buddha on the issue yielded fruit: the Buddha immediately banned the recruitment into his sangha of those involved in the essential state services of Magadha's king.[11]

---

[10] Ibid., V.5, pp. 73–4
[11] Ibid., Mahavagga, I, 40, pp. 194–6.

A less apocalyptic issue was when a jailed robber escaped and wormed his way into the sangha as a monk. As the king had forbidden harm to Buddhist monks, his law-enforcement personnel found themselves in a dilemma. Once again, Bimbisara's discussions with the Buddha resulted in the latter decreeing that criminals must not be admitted to the sangha.[12]

Then there were debtors: some people in debt managed to find refuge in the sangha when escaping the informal bailiffs of the day, and this prompted the Buddha to issue an order that no debtor should be ordained.[13] From these actions it is apparent that the sangha admitted into the order those who were disappointed with the state establishment, but did not hinder the state's policing of its subjects and the martial defence of its territory. With Bimbisara as the earliest royal patron of the Buddhist sangha, these interactions between king and monk body shaped the borderlines between state authority and sangha autonomy.

How to discipline the considerable population of monks with no fixed residence and in need of a regular supply of essentials into a community with a distinct identity was a complicated issue. Bimbisara made suggestions to the Buddha on how to organise the sangha. Having observed that certain other sects of wandering ascetics assembled on certain days each month, he suggested that the Buddha also ask his disciples to gather in regular and well-ordered ways. Heeding this advice, the Buddha asked his monks to assemble on the fourteenth, fifteenth, and eighth day of each month.[14] The dates of these meetings were based on the waning and waxing of the moon in a lunar cycle of 29.5 days. The fourteenth and fifteenth days were not necessarily the same two days each month, and there could be alternative days in each cycle. This rule represented the start of the Uposatha system which designated two to four days in a lunar month for the sangha to gather. As long as the moon waxed and waned, bhikkhus and bhikkhunis everywhere

[12] Ibid., 42, p. 197.
[13] Ibid., 47, p. 199.
[14] Ibid., II, 1, pp. 239–40.

were to observe these days at designated places where they would meet for collective deliberations.

The annual rainy season was of a couple of months' duration and during it travel was difficult, even for well-equipped caravans. The Buddhist sangha thus had to shelter for long stretches in caves or in structures built for them in gardens. Major patrons such as Bimbisara took on the task of providing food to Buddhist monks during the monsoons. There was a fixed date marking the start of the rainy season, with the date varying in different locations depending on the movement of the rain clouds from east to west on the Ganges plain. Monks normally had to observe a schedule at a designated location to which their patron had invited them. For an unspecified reason, Bimbisara once asked the sangha to postpone its rainy season sojourn in his area until the next full moon. The Buddha told his bhikkhus to obey the king's wishes.[15] This can be interpreted as further evidence that the sangha was subject to the needs of the state, even if such needs seemed like the arbitrary commands or desires of a king.

Bimbisara, as we have seen, did not like his soldiers taking refuge in the sangha, nor the sangha harbouring criminals. Conversely, he did not mind and even welcomed the Buddhist sangha's help in taming the rebellious as well as the plunderers of the day, who seem to have been abundant. The names of two robbers of the time exist in the records: a Yakka called Suchiloma, and a forest robber called Angulimala.

The king also found it convenient to have the sangha absorb members of his household or court who grew politically or personally inconvenient: Khema's departure to Venavana was not for the lady's well-being, as given out, but for the rather more serious reason of succession. Ajatasattu may have been the crown prince, but succession was not guaranteed for any prince whose father the king had more than one wife and one adult son. Eventually, Bimbisara was assassinated by Ajatasattu, the very son born of the

---

[15] Ibid., III, 4, p. 301.

Kosala princess. The event is profusely recorded in the Buddhist literature and became legendary among Buddhist devotees worldwide because the ramifications of the assassination went beyond monarchical succession and had a bearing on how Buddhist institutions should be structured.

The story goes that Ajatasattu plotted with Devadatta, a member of the Buddhist sangha and kinsman of the Buddha's Sakya Ganasangha, to kill Ajatasattu's father Bimbisara. As his reward to Devadatta, Ajatasattu would help Devadatta replace the Buddha and become leader of the sangha. Ajatasattu was insecure and impatient to be king, and Devadatta wanted equally to be the sangha's leader. It seems from this that though many Sakyans had joined the sangha when the Buddha gained fame, not all of them had fully grasped the essence of his teachings. Devadatta was one of these malcontents. He had apparently learned certain magic skills to demonstrate his supernatural power. Even though the Buddha frowned on the practice of magic (*iddhi*), Devadatta won admiration among some of his fellow bhikkhus, including the outstanding disciple Sariputta.[16]

Once, the Buddha being in Kosambi with his followers, Devadatta took the opportunity to travel to Rajagaha to win the favour of Prince Ajatasattu with his magic tricks.[17] When the Buddha returned from Kosambi to Venuvana in Rajagaha, Devadatta, with the prince as his patron, made this request in front of a big audience – which included the king and his retinue – to take over the sangha: "The Blessed One, Lord, is now grown aged, he is old and stricken in years, he has accomplished a long journey, and his term of life is nearly run. Let the Blessed One now dwell at ease in the enjoyment of happiness reached even in this world. Let the Blessed One give up the Bhikkhu-sangha to me, I will be its leader."[18] The Buddha dismissed this out of hand, but Devadatta reiterated his desire. Then the Buddha condemned him outright, saying: "I

[16] *Vinaya Texts*, pt III, Cullavagga, VII, 3, 2, pp. 239–40.
[17] Ibid., pp. 233–4.
[18] Ibid., 3, 1, p. 238.

would not give over the Bhikkhu sangha, Devadatta, even to Sariputta and Moggallana. How much less, then, to so vile and evil-loving a person as you."[19] Following up on this, the Buddha sent Sariputta to proclaim throughout the city of Rajagaha that Devadatta had been discredited as a member of the sangha.[20]

This conflict between the Buddha and Devadatta resembles at one level the succession politics of monarchy in a Magadhan kingdom, but in fact it went deeper. The Buddha and Devadatta differed in their ideology, not only in relation to the performance of magic but also in their vision of the sangha. The Buddha did not want to make the sangha in the mould of a monarchy, but rather on the lines of a ganasangha, in which there was no single autocratic leader ruling an established institution. What he wanted was that no specific individual take over the leadership after him – not even the most outstanding of his disciples. His teaching alone was to be the guide for Buddhists of the future.

In order to get Ajatasattu's support to implement his plan to take over the sangha, Devadatta seems to have persuaded the prince to get rid of his father and usurp the throne with this argument: "In former days, prince, people were long-lived, but now their term of life is short. It is quite possible, therefore, that you may complete your time while you are still a prince. So do you, prince, kill your father, and become the Raja; and I will kill the Blessed One, and become the Buddha."[21]

The Pali Buddhist literature contains varying accounts of what exactly happened to Bimbisara. In the *Vinaya* texts, Bimbisara, after learning of the plot, gracefully abdicates the throne to Ajatasattu.[22] In the *Dīgha Nikāya*, Ajatasattu, after Devadatta's demise, confesses to the Buddha that he murdered his father Bimbisara.[23] Whatever the truth of Bimbisara's end as monarch, with Ajatasattu on the throne

---

[19] Ibid., 3, 2, p. 239.
[20] Ibid., p. 240.
[21] Ibid., 3, 4, p. 241.
[22] Ibid., VII, 3, 6, pp. 242–3.
[23] *Dīgha Nikāya*, II, *Sāmañña-phala Sutta*, 99, p. 94.

of Magadha Devadatta made several efforts to kill the Buddha. However, those sent to kill the Buddha all backed off when facing the Blessed One. Even a notoriously fierce elephant called Nalagiri from the king's stable was tamed when he appeared in front of the Buddha.

Failing to assassinate the Buddha, Devadatta tried to create dissensions among the bhikkhus. The assassin *manqué* died, probably of exhaustion, after leading a group of monks out of the sangha. Sariputta and Moggallana persuaded his followers to return to the Buddha.[24] The dissension initiated by Devadatta did not shake the authority of the Buddha within the sangha; on the contrary, it probably further convinced the Buddha that no individual chief should lead the sangha after him.

Devadatta's failure and death were of more consequence to Ajatasattu. Having lost his confidant while inheriting a regime built by his father – who had so conspicuously leaned towards Buddhism more than towards any other religious sect – Ajatasattu felt he had to recalibrate his relationship with the Buddha. It is said that on a full-moon night when the water lily bloomed, Ajatasattu, troubled by his conscience and surrounded by his ministers, solicited their suggestions for a suitable spiritual guide. He dismissed the names of several religious teachers and then questioned Jivaka the physician, who was sitting silently in the audience. As Bimbisara's royal physician and the royal Abhaya's foundling he knew everything there was to know about the court. Ajatasattu had retained him on account of his reputation and medical skill, and Jivaka now told the king that the Buddha, who happened to be staying in his mango grove, could prove an insightful spiritual guide. Ajatasattu took up the suggestion and, riding on his royal elephant while thronged by 500 palace women holding torches and atop 500 female elephants, proceeded to Jivaka's mango grove. Approaching it the king grew nervous at the thought that Jivaka was tricking him into an ambush. The suspicion was dispelled when

---

[24] *Vinaya Texts*, pt III, Cullavagga, VII, 3, 6–14, 3, pp. 243–58.

he discerned the Buddha among the meditating monks: a full-moon night was, very likely, the Uposatha date for the gathering of the Buddha's sangha. After a long dialogue with the Buddha, the king confessed: "Sin had overcome me, Lord, weak and foolish as I am, in that, for the sake of sovereignty, I put to death my father, that righteous man, that righteous king! May the Blessed One accept it of me, Lord, that I acknowledge it as a sin to the end, so that in future I may restrain myself."[25] Ajatasattu's confession to the Buddha is memorialised on the Bharhut Stupa (Fig. 8).

The confession was in the nature of a rapprochement. It represented a reconciliation between the monarchy and the sangha. However, the rapport between monarch and spiritual leader that characterised relations between Bimbisara and the Buddha was over. The young and energetic Ajatasattu first engaged in wars against Kosala and his uncle Pasenadi, and then in a conquest of the Vajji Confederation. Over those years the Buddha probably stayed more in the caves around Vulture's Peak in the mountains outside Rajagaha, rather than in Venavana.

Pasenadi of Kosala, who lived longer than Bimbisara, was an old king when he had to deal with Ajatasattu, his nephew and sometime ally. Kosala was a kingdom as powerful as Magadha. Pasenadi's territory extended from old Kosala to Kasi (Kashi), a city on the Ganges adjacent to Magadha. That is to say, Pasenadi's Kosala dominated the middle Gangetic plain, from the foothills of the Himalaya down to the banks of the Ganges. To the north, several small ganasanghas, including the Sakyas, were perched on the highlands of the Himalayan foothills. Pasenadi, though a patron of the Buddha, was also as king of Kosala ruling a core region of the Brahmanical tradition. He reportedly hired Braham priests to perform Vedic rituals for royal ceremonies, and as reward for their services granted villages or forest lands to the Brahmans for personal or religious use.

Once Buddhism had found a foothold in Kosala, the Buddha and his sangha engaged in serious debates with Brahmans. One

---

[25] *Dīgha Nikāya*, II, *Sāmañña-phala Sutta*, 1–99, pp. 65–94.

Fig. 8: Ajatasattu worshipping the Lord. The Buddha is represented here by a pair of sandals. Courtesy, Indian Museum, Calcutta, nos 184–5, American Institute of Indian Studies, IIS neg. no. 484.78.

such debate, set up between the Buddha on the one hand and the Brahman Pokkarasadi and his disciple Ambattha on the other, was held in a Brahman village called Icchanankala. The debate was focused on comparing the status of Brahmans vis-à-vis that of Ksatriyas, the latter being upheld as superior by the ganasangha ruling elites, including the Sakya and the Licchavi. The lengthy debate seems to have confirmed the superiority of Sakya Ksatriyas over

Brahmans, while also revealing that both groups were commonly involved in intermarriages with other communities: this was apparent because it posed the question of whether sons born of such intermarriages should assume the status of their fathers or their mothers.[26] This and other such debates show that winning the support of Pasenadi by the Buddha required more effort than had been the case with Bimbisara of Magadha, where the sage's heterodoxy had prevailed in the "eastern country" located on the fringes of mainstream Brahmanism.

In the financially and culturally affluent capital city of Savatthi, gahapatis brought in goods as well as religious teachers. We have seen Anathapindika, the famous lay follower of the Buddha who purchased Jetavana from Jeta of Kosala and made it a centre of activity for the sangha. Though other patrons, including Mallika the chief queen, also provided shelters for the sangha, the Buddha's preferred location was Jetavana whenever he was in the vicinity of Savatthi. Equally important in the Kosala territory was Visakha, the businesswoman whom we met earlier. She was one of the lay patrons who helped shape the sangha into an institution, mediating occasionally between the monarchy and the order.

As in Magadha, the rainy season assembly was an important ritual event in the Buddhist calendar. Pasenadi wished to make sure that the eminent elders of the sangha spent the rainy season near Savatthi, most likely at Jetavana. He was not all that forgiving when a senior monk, Upannada Sakyaputta, did not show up in the garden habitat despite promising the king he would be there over the season. On learning of his absence the Buddha reprimanded Upannada Sakyaputta and issued a new rule whereby bhikkhus had to locate themselves in line with what they had promised their patron.[27]

Jetavana was, it seems, a location not only for monks to sojourn in but also where new members were recruited. A grandson

---

[26] Ibid., I, III, *Ambattha Sutta*.
[27] *Vinaya Texts*, Mahāvagga III, 14, pp. 321–4.

of Visakha wanted to join the sangha over a rainy season, but the local sangha's rule was that no ordination could take place during the rains. By the time the rains had ended, however, the boy had lost interest in signing on. Visakha was very upset by this rule that had thwarted her grandson, and someone informed the Buddha of her dismay, which then persuaded the sangha in the Savatthi region to rescind its rule against ordaining recruits during the rainy season.[28]

Some officials who had long served the king took refuge in the sangha and stayed in Jetavana for their remaining years. It was said that after Ajatasattu killed his father, Bimbisara's queen, who was one of Pasenadi's sisters, soon passed away in grief. Pasenadi then decided that his sister's dowry, a village in Kasi, should be taken back from his unworthy nephew. Thereupon a war broke out between Pasenadi and Ajatasattu. Pasenadi being old and Ajatasattu young and energetic, the former was defeated and almost lost his kingdom. In desperation, Pasenadi sent courtiers to Jetavana to get suggestions from the bhikkhus. The courtiers there overheard conversations between two elders – who happened to be former officials of the court – discussing war strategies. Using what had been overheard, Pasenadi managed to overcome Ajatasattu. Eventually, the enemies decided to compromise and Pasenadi sent a daughter, Princess Vajira, to marry the unworthy Ajatasattu, and with the same village of Kasi as her dowry.[29] The details of the legend are naturally impossible to verify, but the featuring within them of Jetavana as a location where the monarch could gain insights and information on strategic issues suggests the political importance of this Buddhist base. It was perhaps where disaffected officials and those who had lost their positions in Savatthi would retreat. And though it seems odd for a Buddhist shelter to provide refuge to those involved in waging war, Jetavana was all the same a place for

---

[28] Ibid., 13, pp. 320–1.
[29] *Jataka Stories*, vol. II, no. 283, p. 275; idem, vol. IV, no. 492, pp. 216–17.

many with experience of the secular world where they discussed matters that were other than spiritual.

The presence of the Buddha and his sangha seems to have mitigated conflicts caused by the expansion of farmlands into tropical forests where indigenous tribes lived. The Kosala monarchy had to protect its rural populations and agrarian revenue by curbing robbers from dashing around and harassing farmers in the woods of the Ganges region. Angulimala, a famous robber of the forest, was tamed by the Buddha and joined the sangha. He was one of the notable examples of forest dwellers entering mainstream society via the Buddhist sangha, which came as a great relief to Pasenadi. However, it was said that Angulimala continued wearing his notorious emblem – a wreath made of the fingers of people he had killed, which gave him his name, "Angulimala" (lit.: finger necklace). Judging from artworks referring to forest chiefs, including Angulimala, this "crown" was more probably a wreath of tree leaves, and thus an emblem of forest people.[30]

The mere existence and apparel of forest people seem to have alarmed those living in sedentary state society. The Buddha banned forest-derived monks wearing emblems of their previous territories and occupation to calm the sangha and village or city residents.[31] The rule that erased signs of their origins and earlier occupations was a step in the Buddhist dress code which distinguished the sangha from others.

The strongest link between Pasenadi and the Buddha was his queen Mallika, a girl who made flower wreaths and encounters the distressed king soon after his defeat by Ajatasattu. Mallika was a follower of the Buddha who often took the Buddha's side when conflicting views by Brahman priests puzzled the king. Pasenadi could not have been young when he married Mallika as Ajatasattu had by then gained the throne. All the same, Pasenadi made Mallika his chief queen as well as laboured strenuously to ensure she

---

[30] Brancaccio, "Aṅgulimāla or the Taming of the Forest", pp. 105–18.
[31] *Vinaya Texts*, Mahāvagga I, 41, p. 196.

presented him with a male heir. Unfortunately, Mallika conceived a girl, and the Buddha, hearing of the king's disappointment, consoled him with the thought that a girl could grow up wise and virtuous and make a good wife for another king and then bring forth more great kings.[32] The princess he was referring to was probably Vajira who, when grown, was sent to placate Ajatasattu, her cousin. Vajira certainly served her father as well as the Kosala kingdom more than did her elder brother Vidudabha.

Like all kings, Pasenadi was desperate to beget a male heir. He very likely had several queens and at least one son, Jeta, whom we have met as the prince who sold Jetavana to Anathapindika. However, in order to elevate his status as a true Ksatriya, Pasenadi asked for the hand of a princess from the Sakya Ganasangha. Wanting to keep their blood "pure", the Sakyans, instead of giving him a girl born of a Sakya father and a Sakya mother, sent him a girl born of a Sakya raja and a slave girl. This daughter, Vassabha Khattiya, was married to Pasenadi and gave birth to Vidudabha, who grew up as a prince of Kosala. However, when Pasenadi discovered Vassabha's lack of pedigree, he condemned both the mother, Vassabha, and her son, Vidudabha, to slavery. The Buddha, however, counselled Pasenadi against such inhumanity and said his son ought to be recognised as a Ksatriya because his father and maternal grandfather were both Ksatriyas.[33] Pasenadi thereupon restored to dignity both mother and son, but his bitterness towards the Sakyans for their duplicity persisted.

Vidudabha was the military commander of Kosala when Mallika became the chief queen and gave birth to Princess Vajira.[34] Unfortunately for Pasenadi, Mallika died early, so that the king

---

[32] *Sanyutta Nikaya,* pt I, III, 2, §6, pp. 110–11.

[33] The story of the conflicts between the Kosala and Sakya ganasanghas is in no. 465 of *Jataka Stories*, vol. iv, pp. 91–6. The similar outline of the story, except for the last part where Vidudabha annihilates the Sakya Ganasangha, appears in the *Rajavagga* (on Kings) in the *Majjhima-Nikaya* IV, 81–90, pp. 243–314.

[34] *Majjhima-Nikāya*, vol. II.ii, 109–11, pp. 294–6.

lost his confidante and wise adviser. Pasenadi's own demise is not widely recorded in Pali texts in the way that Bimbisara's is. One account says that Pasenadi had a loyal and capable commander-in-chief, Bandhula, killed mistakenly, and then experienced remorse for the deed. So Pasenadi then gave the position of commander to Bandhula's nephew, Digha Karayana, to compensate the family. Digha Karayana, however, nursed the family's resentment against the king's misdeed.

At one point, when Pasenadi happened to camp within the territory of the Sakya Ganasangha somewhere in the vicinity of the Buddha, he entrusted his royal insignia – sword, umbrella, diadem, slippers, and fan – to Karayana, while going off himself to meet the Buddha. Over this duration Karayana took the royal insignia to Vidudabha and made him king, leaving only a horse and female servant for Pasenandi. When he emerged from the Buddha's chamber, Pasenadi discovered the betrayal and rode to Rajagaha, hoping his nephew Ajatasattu would help him regain the throne, but died of exhaustion outside the city.[35] Whether Vidudabha was implicated in the coup or not, he became king of Kosala and soon started a campaign to conquer the Sakya Ganasangha.

The Buddha failed to prevent the destruction of the Sakya Ganasangha. However, he attributed the catastrophe partially to the Sakyan obsession with blood purity. Within the political shenanigans of his time the Buddha generally went along with the monarchical system of male primogeniture, and male inheritance more generally. However, he seems to have felt that the status of just the father should suffice to elevate both child and mother to Ksatriya status. Vidudabha, the king of Kosala, never appears in Pali texts after his conquest of the Sakya Ganasangha. He was never in harmony with the Buddhist sangha, as Ajatasattu was in Magadha. Though continuing military conquests against the wishes of the Buddha, Ajatasattu was deferential with the Buddha and consulted him before his major military campaigns.

[35] *Jataka Stories*, vol. IV, no. 465, pp. 95–6.

The last major military action the Buddha witnessed was Magadha's conquest of the Vajji Confederation. The Licchavis were the dominant ganasangha in this confederation and laid claims to the highest Ksatriya status. The rajas of Licchavi were as, if not more, proud Ksatriya elites, and as concerned with their ritual purity as the Sakyans. A ritual tank in Vesali city was where all Licchavi rajas baptised their princes as kings: "By the tank there was set a strong guard, within and without; above it was spread an iron net; not even a bird could find room to get through."[36] The Licchavi lineage survived in historical records all the way down to the Gupta period, and the tank as symbol of their pure Ksatriya status also survived long, at least into the early seventh century: the Chinese Buddhist Xuanzang who visited Vesali described the condition of the tank.[37] Modern archaeological excavation of the tank matches Xuanzang's eyewitness account.[38] This water ritual simultaneously made the Licchavi rajas equal in status among themselves while enabling them to claim a status higher than that of rajas elsewhere.

There were other members of the Vajji Confederation, such as the Videhas of Mithila, the Nayas of Kundapura, and the Mallas of Rapa and Kusinara. After Vidudabha came to power in Kosala and war broke out between him and Ajatasattu over the Kasi–Kosala region, the chiefs of the region could have joined the Vajji Ganasangha.[39] The constituents of the confederation tended to change according to the power dynamic of the time – in fact it remains a question whether Vajji was the name of the confederation or of just one of its constituents. One incident which indicates that the name Vajji was of a well-established and civilised state occurs in the Pali texts. It relates to a time when the Buddha stayed in a garden habitat, within the famous gabled hall of Mahavana frequented by residents of Vesali.

[36] Ibid., p. 94
[37] Xuanzang & Bianji, *Da Tang Xiyuji Jiaozhu*, p. 590.
[38] Falk, *Asokan Sites and Artefacts*, pp. 220–1.
[39] Sharma, *Republics in Ancient India*, p. 84.

Now at that time a company of Licchavi young men were out stalking and ranging in Mahavana; they had their bows strung and were surrounded by a pack of dogs; and they saw the Exalted One seated at the foot of the tree. Then at that sight they cast aside their bows, called off their dogs and approached the Exalted One, saluted him and stood with hands upraised in Silence reverencing him.[40]

Witness to and surprised by this scene was a Licchavi named Mahanama who happened to be exercising in the garden. He rushed to the Buddha, saluted him, and sat down to tell him excitedly how Licchavi youths became Vajjians: "Lord, these Licchavi young men are quick-tempered, rough, greedy fellows . . . they go about plundering and eating; they slap the women and the girls of the clan on their backs. Such are these fellows who now with upraised hands stand in silence reverencing the Exalted One."[41] In this scene the rough and hot-headed Licchavis are tamed by the Buddha into becoming members of the Vajjian Confederation – a larger and more polished political entity that united the militant Licchavis with other more civilised members.

The Vajji Confederation, despite changing its configuration at various points in time, was a formidable economic and military power among the new states of the North Indian plains. Vesali was the capital of the Licchavis and the Vajji Confedederation, and its bustling commercial transactions and cultural events attracted visitors. It was also the home of Mahavira, the founder of Jainism. The Vajjians did not, however, have any single overarching ruler offering patronage to the Buddhist sangha.

A famous welcoming presence for the Buddha in the city was Ambapali, already noted as the chief courtesan who hosted large feasts for the Buddha and his sangha, facilitating a forum for the Buddha's teachings. She also first gave her garden and later her own house to the Buddhist sangha. Outside the city of Vesali were several vanas (gardens) that served as commons for various sects of ascetics. In these shared spaces the Buddha and his best disciples

---

[40] *Anguttara-Nikāya*, vol. III, viii, 58, p. 62.
[41] Ibid., pp. 62–3.

gave lectures and debated their ideas with the followers of other schools.

There is no evidence of direct contact between the Buddha and Mahavira: the latter was probably older and thus out of the picture by the time the Buddha reached Vesali. In the Vajjian country were plenty of followers of Mahavira who seem to have countered the Buddha in debates, mostly in a polite manner. A man named Saccaka, the son of Jains – presumably he himself was also a Jain – liked to engage in these debates. At least twice he summoned 500 Licchavis, a conventional number, to open debates on philosophical questions such as "self (*atman*) and [the] material [world]" with Buddha and his disciples. The Buddhist texts end with his silence and offerings of food to the sangha. There is, however, no indication that Saccaka was converted.[42]

In the gabled hall of Mahavana the Buddha discussed matters with certain naked ascetics who lived in Vesali. These ascetics could have been Jains, who were stricter about ahimsa than the Buddhists.[43] A Licchavi man named Bhaddiya is reported to have frequently appeared in Mahavana to politely ask Buddha many questions. He had heard that the Buddha was skilled in magic tricks and thus asked the sage if the tricks were performed to attract followers. The Buddha lectured him on his major doctrines and dismissed magic tricks as a trivial skill that could mislead people.[44]

A son of the Licchavis, Sunakkhatta, joined the Buddhist sangha but then left it because he held differing opinions. This Sunakkhatta returned several times to debate the Buddha, who called him foolish, but their relationship never deteriorated into hostility – unlike the Buddha's with Devadatta in Magadha.[45] The encounters between the Buddhist sangha and the Jains and other schools active

---

[42] *Majjhima-Nikāya*, vol. I, 35, *Cūlsaccakasutta*, pp. 280–91; 36 *Mahāsaccakasutta*, pp. 291–305.

[43] *Dīgha Nikāya*, vol. III, 1, 11, p 14; *Anguttara-Nikāya*, vol. I, §74, pp. 200–2.

[44] *Anguttara-Nikāya*, vol. II, §iii (193), *Bhaddiya*, pp. 200–4.

[45] *Majjhima-Nikāya*, vol. III, II 252–66, pp. 37–51; vol. I, 1, 67–9, pp. 91–2.

in the Vajjian region, in short, gave the Buddha and his disciples a platform to define their doctrines and sharpen their arguments.

When Ajatasattu decided to conquer the Vajjians, the Buddha wanted the Vajjians to hold fast to their confederation to resist the conquest. Ajatasattu sent his Brahman prime minister Vassakara to Vulture's Peak outside Rajagaha, to meet the Buddha. Respectfully, Vassakara delivered the king's request that he predict the result of the coming warfare. Instead of replying Vassakara, the Buddha conversed with his principal disciple Ananda about the readiness of the Vajjians to resist the Magadhans. He was heard saying that if the Vajjians kept their tradition of convening regularly, stayed unified, worshipped at their shrines, and did not allow diplomacy to break their alliance, they could not be defeated in the battlefield.[46] In the event, Vassakara did resort to the wiles of diplomacy to splinter the Vajjians, and Ajatasattu eventually conquered them.

Despite pushing ahead with his military conquest against the Buddha's message of peace, Ajatasattu managed till the end to keep his reputation as a follower of the Buddha, even claiming, as a Ksatriya, a share in the relics of the Buddha.[47] Nevertheless, Ajatasattu was not the ideal king from the Buddha's perspective, and a far cry from the cakkavattin (cakravartin in Sanskrit), the king who turned the wheel of dhamma. This period of the rise of states in North India was when the Vedic lineages had almost disappeared from politics. Candravamsha, the lunar lineage, had ended with infighting – as signalled by the story of the Mahabharata. The kings of Kosala, though ruling over the land of the ancient and sacred king Rama, could hardly claim any legacy from that idealised ruler. Kings across the subcontinent at the time of the Buddha originated in obscure families but aspired and usually came to acquire Ksatriya status. They made strategic marriage alliances to promote their status as well as to facilitate military conquests. The ganasanghas, however, tried to cling to the Vedic lineage myth and practised strict endogamy as a mark of their distinction.

---

[46] *Dīgha Nikāya*, vol. II, 72–6, pp. 78–81.
[47] Ibid., 164, p. 187.

Sakyamuni of the Sakya Ganasangha can thus be sensed as having a greater affinity with the ganasangha polities, even if he critiqued them. The legendary Rama, seen as the ideal benevolent king by the Brahmanical tradition, had struggled and won the throne to assert the rule of primogeniture. Trying to win support from a variety of rulers, the Buddhists had to deal with the Rama tradition. One Dasaratha story in the jatakas is a version of the Buddhist interpretation of royal primogeniture.[48] In it the two princes, Rama and Lakkhana, as well as the princess Sita, are all siblings, and Sita eventually becomes Rama's queen. Their place of exile is the Himalaya instead of the Deccan forest to the south of the Ganges – as in the classic version of the epic Ramayana. The *Dasaratha Jataka* story ends with Rama ascending the throne as the eldest son, the very idea upheld in the Ramayana. Buddhists, it seems, agreed that primogeniture was the ideal succession rule for monarchy. On the other hand, despite their clannish inbreeding, their affinities were with the unmonarchic ganasangha polities. Beyond this contradiction lay the sangha's relative helplessness: it was witness to regular events of patricide in the monarchies, and to human suffering from the constant warfare among varying political entities, but all the sangha could do was provide refuge to those who were losers and the victims of warfare. The sangha's appeal lay to a considerable measure in its sheltering function, its implicit statement that, for all the differences in the format of contemporary politics, the common ground to which they all gave rise was human suffering, and thus that for the common person the provision of succour rather than the acquisition of power was what really mattered.

[48] *Jataka Stories,* vol. IV, no. 461, pp. 78–82.

6

Queens and the Buddhist Sangha

Ambapali, Stateswoman of the Vajji Ganasangha

EVEN IN HER OLD AGE, Ambapali was beautiful. Though her face was lined with wrinkles, her eyes were bright. After walking around the cetiya – a shrine symbolising the presence of the Buddha – in a procession of like-minded followers, she would sit under a tree in a mango orchard and sink into deep thought. Scrutinising her withered skin, she would contemplate the vicissitudes of her eventful, and sometimes volatile, life.

When she was young, Ambapali's beauty and talent had been recognised not only in Vesali but in all the cities of the Ganges plain. At the time of her birth in Vesali these cities were still new and vigorous and she had grown to become a famous public figure in the most cosmopolitan city of the day – a city that was swept up in a storm that forever shaped the future of North Indian society.

Ambapali and the Buddha, as we have seen, were contemporaries. During their lifetime a system of lineage-based pastoral-agricultural societies had made way for territorial states with cities as both centres of trade and capitals of the new political structures. As the capital of the Licchavis – the most powerful of the nine states grouped within the Vajji Confederation – Vesali was the grandest of them all. Buddhist writers of the time said that the Vajji Confederation itself was one of sixteen powerful states on the Gangetic plain, and they also remarked on its structural difference from the other great powers. It was not ruled by a king (raja), but by a confederation of ganasanghas. *Gana* means numerous and denotes the mass, and *sangha* means a gathering. Thus, literally, ganasangha meant a gathering of the populace.

There were several ganasanghas during the middle of the first millennium BCE, the Sakya Ganasangha in the Himalayan foothills being one such. However, within all the ganasanghas, only the city of Vesali ranked among the largest cities of the era, and only the Vajji Confederation could match its power against the most powerful nearby kingdoms, Kosala and Magadha.

The cities of North India were similar to Athens and other ancient Greek cities in that not everyone living within them had equal political rights. As in Greece, in the ganasanghas women had no say in public affairs. Only adult males who were the heads of households had full rights to decide on the momentous matters of the day. Such men were also called "raja" to denote their rule over their domestic "kingdom". A small ganasangha such as that of the Sakyas contained about 500 rajas. In Vesali, as noted earlier, it was conversationally commonplace to refer to the 7707 Licchavi rajas within it. Though these numbers were certainly clichés, they do indicate an extraordinary difference in the sizes of cities at the time.

The total population of a city was of course much larger than the number of fully empowered rajas: women, children, and young adult males waiting for their chance to become the raja of a Licchavi lineage were also residents, and not all the residents of Vesali belonged to a Licchavi lineage. Cities being places of opportunity for people from a variety of different backgrounds, non-citizens, itinerants, and a labouring class would almost certainly have greatly outnumbered the rajas and their families. Though these outsiders could not join the Licchavis in voting on public matters, they could find jobs, start businesses, and engage in trade and commerce. Cities have also always afforded anonymity, enabling the socially disadvantaged to incrementally shed aspects of their tribal or village status in some proportion with their acquisition of wealth and possessions.

The breaching of caste walls via urban social mobility was not limited to urban newcomers. In Magadha, when military men gained power and called themselves rajas, it would have been dangerous to question their caste status at birth. The Licchavis, the ruling elites of Vesali and the Vajji Confederacy, claimed descent from the Solar Lineage, reckoned as one of the two most prestigious Ksatriya lineages. While the Licchavis lived in Vesali and managed their public affairs collectively through discussion, debate, ceremonies, and the election of a chief raja and administrators, the Magadha monarchy ruled from Rajagaha and claimed for themselves the most fertile rice-paddy lands, iron-ore mines, and the elephants that roamed the forests. Even as traders and professionals travelled from city to city, the rajas in Vesali and the raja in Rajagaha watched every political move of their rivals.

This was the context in which Ambapali was born in Vesali. Her family status at the time of her birth was not traceable: it was said that she had appeared suddenly in the mango orchard of the chief raja's gardens.[1] The gardener who found her presented her to the Licchavi rajas. The ganasangha, stunned by her beauty, voted to ensure that she was not married off to any single man. Instead, they elected her as the official hostess and courtesan of the city.

It is obviously impossible to ascertain how much truth there is to such a legend of origins, but we do know that she was not of a high caste and that she offered no credentials indicating her affiliation with any caste. Had she appeared in a kingdom such as Magadha, Ambapali would have been taken by the king's men to the king and made one of his concubines. In Vesali, which was less autocratic – or at least more democratically autocratic – it was not for the chief raja to decide whom she must marry or be gifted to, the entire ganasangha had to decide. According to the lore on how she acquired her unique position, the ganasangha – presumably fearing that many of its rajas would covet such a beauty – decided that marrying her to anyone at all was much too risky. The way out was to make her "queen" of the entire city.

---

[1] *Therīgāthā*, commentary, p. 120.

Ambapali's anointment as "queen" of the Licchavis was a major event celebrated at the city's annual spring festival. This was the occasion when the Licchavis held a ceremony to elect the chief raja and anoint the uparajas (princes) who would succeed their deceased or elderly fathers as full-fledged rajas. The newly elected chief raja and the young rajas were then given a ceremonial bath in a large tank built for the purpose. We have no detailed description of it, but it seems plausible that Ambapali's anointment was also done ceremoniously and with fanfare in this tank.[2]

Being the city's public courtesan at Vesali was tricky. Ambapali lived in a highly hierarchical society and the Licchavis, as well as other members of the confederation, were very conscious of their high-caste status. Ambapali herself, by contrast, was of indeterminate family background, her parentage obliterated, probably deliberately, by the Vesali citizenry. But in the urban environment it was money that talked and Ambapali is known to have lived an opulent life – she owned a big house, a large mango garden, many horses and wagons, and numerous servants. More importantly, she played hostess to many of the famous people of her time, including the Buddha.

The middle of the first millennium BCE was conducive to religious thought in North India, and Vesali was a city much favoured by non-conventional thinkers. Mahavira was born in Vesali and, like his close contemporary the Buddha, was critical of orthodox Brahman rituals and social ordering. That the two most important anti-orthodox thinkers of this time came from the ganasangha polities was not an accident. Both Jainism and Buddhism referred to their believers as comprising a sangha – an obvious borrowing from ganasangha. Originally, the term sangha, as used by both Jains and Buddhists, did not refer to monasteries – that being a later semantic development. In the time of the Buddha the sangha was a group of monks and nuns following their leaders from one city to another city to preach and be fed by hosts and audiences. Vesali, with its sizeable population, was host to a number of itinerant preachers and teachers.

[2] Sharma, *Republics in Ancient India*, pp. 104–5.

The arrival of the Buddha at Kotigama, a village near Vesali, was big news to residents of the city. Ambapali ordered a train of her magnificent wagons to be made ready and rode in one of them in procession to the village. When her carriage reached the point where the passage for vehicles ended, she alighted and walked to where the Buddha was seated. She saluted him respectfully and sat near him to listen to what he was teaching. When he had finished his lecture Ambapali said: "Might the Blessed One, Lord, consent to take his meal with me tomorrow together with the fraternity of bhikkhus . . ."[3] The Buddha silently indicated assent. Ambapali saluted, went round him with her right side respectfully towards him, and departed.

On her way back to Vesali, Ambapali came up against a great host of wagons driven by young male Licchavis, "pole to pole, yoke to yoke, wheel to wheel, and axle to axle." When they inquired about her trip, Ambapali proudly told them that the Buddha had accepted her invitation to bring his entire sangha to her garden for a meal. The young Licchavis, all dressed up for their opportunity to meet the Buddha, were so envious that they made haste to the place where the Buddha dwelt to offer their own invitation. The Buddha, however, declined them since he had already accepted Ambapali's offer.

The next day Ambapali prepared a big feast in her garden and sat near the Buddha while those in the sangha took their meal. When the meal was over, she declared she was donating the garden to the Buddha and his sangha. The Buddha accepted her offer and then gave a lecture on the doctrines of Buddhism right there in her garden. Thereafter the Ambapali Garden became one of the properties where Buddhist monks and nuns could visit and stay. More than a thousand years later the Chinese Buddhist Xuanzang, on his visit to Vesali, said the Ambapali Garden was still clearly marked.[4]

---

[3] The story is from one of the earliest Buddhist texts: *Vinaya Texts*, VI, 30, pp. 1–5.

[4] Xuanzang, *Da Tang Xiyu Ji Jiaozhu*, p. 593.

On a later occasion, when the Buddha returned to Vesali he is said to have stayed at the Ambapali Garden.⁵ Once again Ambapali went off to invite the Buddha and his sangha to a meal at her home and the Buddha again accepted her invitation. Once again on her way back she ran into young Licchavis racing towards the Ambapali Garden, desperate as ever to host the Buddha. This time round, hearing that the Buddha had again accepted Ambapali's invitation, they offered her a fat sum to allow them the privilege of feeding the Buddha instead. Ambapali refused and the next day a great feast of rice and sweet cakes was held inside her magnificent mansion. When the feast drew to an end, Ambapali had a low stool brought to her and sat on it near the Buddha. On this occasion she declared she was giving her mansion over to the Buddha and his order. This mansion, says Xuanzang, later became a hostel for aged Buddhist nuns who were unable any longer to travel with the sangha through the villages. Various aunts of the Buddha as well as other elderly nuns passed into nirvana in this house.⁶

The Buddha made several more visits to Vesali, staying always at the Ambapali Garden. During his last visit there he predicted his own death. A few months later he passed into nirvana near Kusinagara, a small city to the north-east of Vesali.

Apparently Ambapali did not give up her secular life as Vesali's public courtesan during the lifetime of the Buddha. She seems to have had a good rapport with the sage, their mutual understanding jealously watched by young male Licchavis. Despite their envy, the Licchavis allowed Ambapali to be the favoured hostess of the Buddha in their city. There remains the suspicion that Ambapali's feasts and donations were not motivated entirely by her own piety. These events took place during a time of intense warfare, and they may well have been part of the diplomatic manoeuvres undertaken on behalf of the city of Vesali and the Vajji Confederation. Evidently,

---

⁵ This story is from the *Mahā Parinibbāna Suttanta*, which is collected in the *Dīgha Nikāya* and *Vinaya*, both being parts of the earliest Buddhist texts. See *Dīgha Nikāya*, D.ii, pp. 94–8.

⁶ Xuanzang, *Da Tang Xiyu Ji Jiaozhu*, p. 591.

despite the hostility of their sons, Ambapali enjoyed the support of the Licchavi rajas.

Living in an age of uncertainty and rapid change, Ambapali is likely to have been attracted to teachings which spoke of the transient nature of material wealth, and in particular physical beauty. During her own time of prosperity she saw people who, coming into Vesali to find a better life, become important householders who came to own large caravans and vast trading networks; on the other hand she saw those whose status was reduced to that of sweepers and whose jobs entailed taking garbage out of the city. Such city dwellers, who had been reduced by misfortune and indigence to clean the city streets, were certainly among the first generations of Indian outcastes, or "untouchables". To see the degradation of such people was also to understand what the Buddha was making visible – the transience and ephemerality of her own wealth and beauty. Better, then, to donate her possessions to the Buddhist order and use her social power to serve a cause larger than herself. She was fortunate too in that the Licchavis and the other Vesali citizens respected her as a figure symbolising the prosperity and honour of their city.

Ambapali and courtesans in other cities such as Salavati in Rajagaha perhaps represent the beginnings of the state-sponsored institution of entertainment. According to Kautilya, by the time of the Mauryan empire a government department specialised in supervising the matriarchal establishment of a courtesan, including slave girls and sons. The king was expected to dispatch a teacher to train courtesans as well as slave girls in music, dance, and theatrical performance. The son of a courtesan who had not been abandoned by his mother was meant to manage stage performances.[7] But when Ambapali was the courtesan of Vesali, her activity represented a totally new phenomenon, a challenge to the social norm even in the new urban culture. A rumour of the time was that even Bimbisara, king of Magadha, made a secret trip to Vesali to meet Ambapali.[8]

[7] *Kautiliya Arthasastra*, 2.27, 1–30.
[8] Sharma, *Republics in Ancient India*, p. 123.

What the Licchavis did expect from Ambapali was assistance in defending their city and way of life, and in this cause, she was their ally in getting the moral support of the Buddha, the most respected wise man of the time.

In the confrontation between the most powerful monarchy and the largest ganasangha, the Buddha clearly took the side of Vesali. When staying in the city he taught the Vajjians the value of discipline, regularity, and cohesion against the might of Magadha. These values, as we have seen, entailed that they should meet regularly as ordained by their tradition and act in concord; they should respect the ancient Vajjian institutions; they should defer to their elders and listen to their advice; they should not violate women against their will; they should make offerings and maintain the old shrines; and they should protect and offer alms to religious recluses.[9] In other words, the Buddha was saying that the Vajjians already had all the institutions needed to keep them strong in the defence of their way of life. These were no different from the principles that the Buddha taught his sangha.[10]

Given his respect for the ganasangha traditions of the Licchavis and the Vajji Confederation, the Buddha made many trips to Vesali to provide moral support and guidance. His interactions with Ambapali make it clear that, though she was a courtesan, he did not see her as one of the common prostitutes who proliferated in the urban areas; on the contrary he treated her as a representative of the Licchavis and of the city of Vesali. The city itself did not succeed in resisting its enemies. As noted earlier, the Vajjians lost against Magadha after the Brahman minister from there, Vassakara, successfully sowed foment in their city.

It was probably sometime after Vesali was conquered by Ajatasattu that Ambapali renounced the mundane world and joined the Buddhist sangha. We do not know where she spent her last days as a nun but it seems logical to presume she continued in the house she had donated to the sangha and which housed elderly sisters.

---

[9] *Dīgha Nikāya,*, D.ii, pp. 74–5.
[10] Ibid., pp. 76–7.

By this time we know that, thanks to Maha Pajapati, the bhikkhuni community was an established institution within the Buddhist sangha.

Maha Pajapati, Matriarch of the Sakya Ganasangha

Buddha had, as noted earlier, been persuaded to give permission to establish a women's community at the persistent request of his aunt and foster mother, the Sakya matriarch Pajapati Gotami, who had pleaded the cause of women being allowed to join the sangha: "It would be well, Lord, if women should be allowed to renounce their homes and enter the homeless state under the doctrine and discipline proclaimed by the Thatagata."[11] The Buddha had at first firmly declined her request but after two more failed attempts Pajapati led a number of Sakya women in the footsteps of the Buddha to Vesali. There she cut off her hair and donned orange robes in the style of bhikkhus. Her feet swollen and clothes dusty after a long journey, weeping tears, she stood outside the preaching hall for the Buddha to heed her plea. Seeing her miserable condition Ananda pleaded her cause, was rebuked, but finally touched an emotional chord:

> If then, Lord, they are capable thereof [of reaching enlightenment], since Maha Pajapati the Gotami has proved herself of great service to the Blessed One, when as aunt and nurse she nourished him and gave him milk, and on the death of his mother suckled the Blessed One at her own breast, it were well, Lord, that women should have permission to go forth from the household life and enter the homeless state, under the doctrine and discipline proclaimed by the Tathagata.[12]

Pajapati was thereafter superintendent of the bhikkhunis and called Maha Pajapati (the Great Pajapati). The Buddha laid out eight major rules for Maha Pajapati to ensure bhikkhuni discipline,

---

[11] *Vinaya Texts,* Cullavagga, X, 1, pp. 320–7. The following story is from this passage.
[12] Ibid., p. 322.

the foremost being that all female adherents respect and obey bhikkhus and seek the protection of bhikkhus. Also, "A Bhikkhuni is not to spend the rainy season in a district in which there are no Bhikkhus."[13] Maha Pajapati implemented these and other such stipulations vigorously. All the same, Sakyamuni seems to have had reservations about his decision to admit women into the sangha, for he confessed to Ananda:

> If, Ananda, women had not received permission to go out from the household life and enter the homeless state, under the doctrine and discipline proclaimed by the Tathāgata, then would the pure religion, Ananda, have lasted long, the good law would have stood fast for a thousand years. But since, Ananda, women have now received that permission, the pure religion, Ananda, will not now last so long, the good law will now stand fast for only five hundred years. Just, Ananda, as houses in which there are many women and but few men are easily violated by burglars; just so, Ananda, under whatever doctrine and discipline women are allowed to go out from the household life into the homeless state, that religion will not last long. And just, Ananda, as when the disease called mildew falls upon a field of rice in fine condition, that field of rice does not continue long . . .[14]

From the early days of his enlightenment, outstanding women had supported Sakyamuni. But given the scale of warfare, unrest, and pillaging, the Buddha's worry was that the admission of female members would make the sangha more vulnerable to attacks. The abusing and attacking of women, especially beautiful young women, was rampant, and for the sangha a definite risk. And there was no escaping the widespread patriarchal view that such women were seductresses who might ruin morals in the sangha. The Buddha's frequent teaching on the evanescence of women's physical beauty, using contemporary beauties as examples, even while seeing them as capable of enlightenment, is one of the contradictions in Buddhist doctrines and institutions that has never been resolved.

[13] Ibid., p. 323.
[14] Ibid., p. 236.

The Pali *Vinaya* text does not specify the time and condition of the Sakya people when Pajapati followed the Buddha to Vesali. But the Sakyas had long been threatened by Pasenadi's powerful monarchy at Kosala – and in fact by several ganasanghas nearby, in addition to the Kosala kings to their south.

It had all started with Pasenadi who, as briefly mentioned earlier, had tried his hand at a marital alliance with the Sakyas – and burned his fingers in the attempt. We can look at this episode in more detail here. Pasenadi considered it expedient to get a bride from the Sakyas as they were believed to be endowed with a solid Ksatriya status. A sign of this was how jealously they guarded their caste status – they did not even share their meals with outsiders, so great was their fear of pollutants. So, when Pasenadi asked for the hand of a Sakya daughter, the entire assembly of rajas was panic-stricken.[15] Pasenadi was a typical monarch of his time in that he had gained power through military prowess and political alliances, not because he was born into a Ksatriya lineage. He had muddied the waters further by marrying women from varying backgrounds: in fact his chief queen, Mallika, whom he had married for her beauty with no regard for her lineage, was the daughter of a garland maker.[16] The Sakya rajas had to gather to deliberate a solution to Pasenadi's proposal. A raja named Mahanama said he could offer his daughter, Vassabha Khattiya, born of a slave mother, to Pasenadi.[17] The Sakya rajas accepted his offer and managed to trick the envoy from Pasenadi into picking up the "princess". In due course, Vassabha Khattiya gave birth to a son, Vidudabha, who enjoyed

---

[15] The story of the conflicts between the Kosala and Sakya ganasanghas is in *Jataka Stories*, no. 465, vol. iv, pp. 91–6. The similar outlines of the story, except for the last part where Vidudabha annihilates the Sakya ganasangha, appears in *Rajavagga* in *Majjhima-Nikaya*, IV, 81–90, pp. 243–314.

[16] According to *Jataka Stories*, no. 415, pp. 244–5, Mallika the garland maker gave the food she carried to work to the Buddha. Having thus acquired merit, she encountered Pasenadi who, startled by her beauty, made her his chief queen.

[17] Other Pali texts refer to her as Vassabha. The Khattiya part (Pali version for Ksatriya) was apparently added to trick Pasenadi.

royal status in Kosala. When Vidudabha grew up he made a visit to his mother's maiden home, where the Sakyas insulted him on account of his mother having been a slave. Humiliated, he returned to the capital, Savatthi, where his father, upon discovering the reason for his son's depressed state, heaped insult on injury: Vassabha Khattiya and Vidudabha were deprived of their royal status and treated as slaves.

The Buddha, a son of the Sakyas, provided crucial mediation by conceding that while the Sakyas were in the wrong for cheating him, Pasenadi as the father should acknowledge his wife and progeny as being of royal blood.[18] Pasenadi thereafter restored both mother and son to their earlier status.

When Vidudabha became king of Kosala, he trained his sights vengefully on the Sakya Ganasangha, and even the Buddha's effort at interception failed to save the caste-conscious Sakyas.[19] The entire edifice of Buddhism being a critique of caste Brahmanism, the Buddha obviously disagreed with the Sakya rajas in their caste consciousness and vanity. His persuasion of Pasenadi to restore the rights of Vassabha Khattiya and Vidudabha show him favouring a patriarchal inheritance principle that superseded the belief in high-caste status among royalty and elites. This may well have seemed a convenient and even felicitous argument to monarchs and rajas who often married beautiful women of low birth.

Vidudabha devastated the Sakyas, though the consequence of his conquest was probably exaggerated in the jataka narrative which states that all Sakya men were slaughtered. Whether the efforts of Maha Pajapati and her women followers from the Sakya Ganasangha took place before or after the Vidudabha military campaign is hard to make out. In either case, the Sakyas had long lived in the shadow of the powerful Kosalas. Warfare had created many widows and mothers who had lost their sons and become destitute. It can be surmised that either the precarious political situation more generally or the post-war devastation caused by Vidudabha

---

[18] *Jataka Stories*, no. 465, p. 93.
[19] Ibid., p. 96.

drove the Sakya women to a state of such desperation that they walked all the way from their homes in the Himalayan foothills to Vesali on the Ganges plain.

Maha Pajapati's greatness cannot be in doubt since she pioneered the establishment of a refuge for women cast out of mainstream society. This institution – of something like a decent option for women who were unmarried or no longer in a marital relationship – also represented a rebellion against the orthodox Brahmanical patriarchy which commodified women by seeing them in mainly functional terms – to marry or give pleasure to men and give birth to children. Bhikkhunis, especially elderly ones such as Ambapali when she joined the sangha, could not travel as easily or as extensively as did the bhikkhus. Safe housing for the sisterhood was a protection from rains as well as marauding men.

Khema, a Queen of Magadha

Many of the bhikkhus and bhikkhunis in the earliest Buddhist sangha composed poems that were subsequently collected to inspire men and women who wanted to join the sangha. Of the bhikkhunis whose psalms were collected, as many as twenty-three were from royal and noble families.[20] These were women who had jettisoned a comfortable material environment to join the sangha for spiritual enlightenment, as well as to escape various forms of political danger. Both Pajapati and Ambapali had run away from ganasanghas destroyed by powerful monarchies. In the political centres of monarchies, power struggles were even more dangerous for women. In them a smooth system of inheritance was the key to strong and lasting power. Patriarchal lineage was the basis of inheritance, and primogeniture the principle seeking to ensure smooth transitions. In the heyday of the two superpowers of the time, Kosala and Magadha, both their leading men Pasenadi and Bimbisara had at least one son each. This was probably why the Buddha could convince Pasenadi to forgive the Sakya rajas and retain Vidudabha

---

[20] Horner, *Women under Primitive Buddhism*, p. 167.

as his heir. Unfortunately for both kings, their sons Vidudabha and Ajatasattu were impatient princes who, rather than await their turn, violently usurped the throne via patricide or paternal imprisonment. In such an environment, the consorts of the kings who "failed" to produce a male offspring were precariously placed.

Khema, an outstanding bhikkhuni reputed for her intelligence and understanding of the Buddha's doctrines, was such a queen: she was beautiful but bore Bimbisara no son. Another queen of Bimbisara, a sister of Pasenadi's, gave birth to Ajatasattu. It was said Khema was aware of her own beauty and had no interest in living the ascetic life. It was her husband who was keener on her departure and led her into the arms of the Buddha's sangha. He cajoled her in that direction by having his people tell her of the floral beauty of Veṇuvana; left to herself, Khema would have exited the garden even before she had met the Buddha, but the king's men restrained her. At this point, the story has it that the Buddha conjured up the vision of a celestial beauty to make Khema's earthly attractiveness seem to her pale by comparison, and then outlined the ageing process to which all beauty was subject by making the celestial apparition come down to earth as a pitiable crone. From this, it was said, Khema realised her own vanity and turned to the teachings of the Buddha.[21]

The enlightenment of Khema is obviously a conventional story of conversion, while the narrative of Bimbisara's inducements to push Khema in the Buddha's direction betrays the harsh truth that Khema's beauty was no insurance for value and status within a royal household if she "failed" her maternal role as male child-bearer. Khema's psalm is written as a rejection of the value placed on physical beauty.[22] She was fortunate in having been born in a noble Kosala family because it saved her skin: Bimbisara could not afford to offend her lineage by getting rid of her brutally. Packing her off to the Buddha was the safe option.

---

[21] Commentary on Khema's psalm, *Therīgāthā*, pp. 81–2.
[22] Ibid., pp. 83–4.

Khema, along with Pasenadi's chief queen Mallika, is cited as one of the model female lay disciples of the Buddha.[23] The earlier emphasis on her earthly beauty is displaced once she joins the sangha by her fame as a bhikkhuni of exceptional intelligence.[24] Hearing of her reputation for wisdom, Pasenadi, brother of her rival queen in Magadha, pays her a visit at a resort near Savatthi and poses a question to her: "How say you, lady: Does the Tathāgata exist after death?"[25] This was a challenging philosophical question. Tathagata literally means "the one who comes and goes" – a name for the itinerant Buddha. The image of the Buddha in continuous passage or in a state of permanent transition suggests not just temporal movement, but also his doctrine of the cycles of rebirth and human aspiration for ultimate arrival into the state of nirvana. The Buddha's comings and goings in the world are regularly used metaphorically in narratives about him to foreground the concept of rebirth. Khema, in her reply to Pasenadi, uses every trick in the book to avoid a direct answer to his question, summarised by her statement that it "is not revealed by the Exalted One." When pressed further by the king, she takes offence:

> "Now in this matter, Maharajah, I will question you. Do you reply as you think fit. Now how say you, Maharajah? Have you some accountant, some ready-reckoner or calculator, able to count the sand in the Ganges, thus: 'There are so many hundred grains, or so many thousand grains, or so many hundreds of thousands of grains of sand?'"
> "No indeed, lady."
> "Then have you some accountant, ready-reckoner or calculator, able to reckon the water in the mighty ocean, thus: 'There are so many gallons of water, so many hundred, so many thousand, so many hundreds of thousand gallons of water?'"
> "No indeed, lady."
> "How is that?"
> "Mighty is the ocean, lady, deep, boundless, unfathomable."

---

[23] *Anguttara-Nikāya*, IV, p. 229.

[24] Numerous references to Khema appear in the early Pali texts. See Horner, *Women under Primitive Buddhism*, pp. 168–9.

[25] *Sanyutta Nikāya*, IV, p. 266.

"Even so, Maharajah, if one should try to define the Tathagata by his bodily form, that bodily form of the Tathagata is abandoned, cut down at the root, made like a palm-tree stump, made something that is not, made of a nature to spring up again in future time. Set free from reckoning as body, Maharajah, is the Tathagata. He is deep, boundless, unfathomable, just like the mighty ocean . . ."[26]

Pasenadi was taken aback by Khema's wit but doubted her authority on this matter. But when he went off to check with the Buddha himself, he found the Buddha replying in exactly the same manner.[27]

Had Khema produced a son who inherited the throne of Magadha, she would have been guaranteed royal status and lived out her life as a queen rather than as a Buddhist theologian. Another of Bimbisara's queens, known as the Princess of Vedeha, was fortunate enough to produce Ajatasattu. This queen from the royal lineage of Kosala was a sister of Pasenadi and one more pawn in the game of marital alliances between political families. As noted already, she had brought as her dowry the village of Kasi. After Ajatasattu's ascent and the confession of his patricide to the Buddha[28] – an event recorded in the earliest Buddhist documents and shown on one of the reliefs of the Bharhut Stupa – his mother fades out of the narrative entirely and no one even knows her name.[29] All we learn of her is that she passed away soon after her husband, and that her dowry was handed down by Pasenadi to his daughter Vajira when she was married off to Ajatasattu to appease that king.[30]

Mallika, Queen of Kosala

Mallika, chief queen of Pasenadi and beautiful daughter of a garland maker, also bore no son for the king but was saved the obloquy

---

[26] Ibid., pp. 266–7.
[27] Ibid., p. 268.
[28] *Samanna-phala Sutta*, in *Dīgha Nikāya*, 47–100, pp. 65–95.
[29] In the Indian Museum, nos 184–5.
[30] *Jataka Stories*, no. 283, commentary, vol. II, p. 275; idem, no. 492, commentary, vol. IV, pp. 216–17.

of being a queen without producing a male child by her early death. Though she did not join the sangha, while at Savatthi she was a staunch ally of the Buddha within the monarchy. The story woven around her is that when at a flower garden to pick flowers for her garlands, she saw the Buddha and his sangha approach and provided them food out of her own portion carried for the working day. This act of charity fetching her merit, the Buddha immediately predicted she would be Pasenadi's chief queen. It so happened that Pasenadi had just lost a battle with Ajatasattu and had retreated to Savatthi. Hearing beautiful singing in the garden, he rode his horse thence, where Mallika, instead of retreating, seized the bridle of the horse. This was the cue for the king to take solace in her lap, and soon thereafter they repaired to his palace for her inauguration as chief queen.[31]

Mallika was apparently not aware that her great merit – gained by giving up her own lunch for the Buddha – had made her the chief queen of Kosala. Her understanding of the Buddha's teaching probably started with a dialogue with him in Jetavana. Perplexed by the sudden fortune of being a queen and facing the challenge of behaving like one, she enquired why some women were endowed with beauty and others not, why some came into the world with a good nature and others with a bad temper, why some were rich and the rest poor. The Buddha explained that a woman's qualities in her former lives determined her current fortune or misfortune. A good person in former lives was reborn as an amicable woman; a generous giver to religious figures was reborn with wealth; a woman not jealous of others would have beauty subsequently. And so on, and vice versa . . . Mallika saw that her present fortune was the result of her own earlier past decencies, and that she had to carry on the good work to guarantee happiness in her future lives:

> Now again, Lord, in this rajah's family there are maids of the nobles, maids of the Brahmins, of the householders too. Over them I hold supremacy. Lord, from this day forth I will indeed become good-tempered, not irritable. Even with great provocation I will not become

[31] *Jataka Stories*, no. 415, commentary, vol. III, pp. 244–5.

upset nor stubborn. I will not show ill-will nor displeasure. I will give to recluse and Brahmin food and drink . . . bed, lodging and light. I will not become jealous-minded. I will not be jealous of other folks' gain, nor of the honour, respect, reverence, homage, and worship paid to them. I will not be revengeful nor will I harbour a grudge.

It is wonderful, Lord! It is marvellous, Lord! Lord, may the Exalted One accept me as a woman disciple from this day forth so long as life may last, as one who has gone to him for refuge.[32]

Mallika followed through on her promise and grew into one of the most loyal lay disciples of the Buddha.[33] As noted, she donated a park for recluses to rest in near Savatthi, where the Buddha often sojourned and engaged in debates.[34] She advised Pasenadi on state matters and managed life in the palace efficiently. She had a daughter and got along with other women as well as with Prince Vidudabha. In a lengthy discussion about one of the teachings of the Buddha with the king, she acted gracefully: the question posed was whether human sorrow arose from affection for loved ones. Pasenadi could not comprehend the logic of the causal connection that was being made, so Mallika asked him: "Is your daughter Vajiri [Vajira] dear to you?" And he replied, "Yes, Mallika. My daughter Vajiri is dear to me." Then, Mallika explained to him that if misfortune befell Vajiri, he would be in deep grief. She then raised the same question about Queen Vassabha and Prince Vidudabha.[35] Using these as examples, she made Pasenadi comprehend the nature of philosophical logic. Her conversation simultaneously reveals that she harboured no jealousy or grudge against other members of the royal family.

It seems, however, that disputes with her husband were inevitable: Mallika and Pasenadi quarrelled so bitterly once that the situation only happened to be saved because the Buddha and his

[32] *Anguttara-Nikāya*, vii (197), pp. 214–18.
[33] Ibid., viii, ix (90), vol. IV, p. 229.
[34] Mallika's garden is referred to several times in the Pali canon, e.g. *Dīgha Nikaya, Potthapada Sutta* 178.1, pt 1, p. 245; *Majjhima-Nikāya*, II, 22–3, p. 222.
[35] *Majjhima-Nikāya*, vol. II, ii, 109–11, pp. 294–6.

sangha came to the palace seeking food. Noticing Mallika's absence when being served, the Buddha enquired after her and the king replied:

> "What have you to do with her, Reverend Sir? . . . Her head is turned, she is intoxicated with the honour she enjoys."
>
> [The Buddha nevertheless reprimanded the king:] "Sire," he said, "after you yourself bestowed this honour on the woman, it is wrong of you now to get rid of her, and not to put up with the offence she has committed against you."
>
> [The king then had the queen come to the Buddha, and both listened to the Buddha's admonition:] "You ought to live together in peace," and singing the praises of the sweets of concord he went his way.[36]

The Buddha seems to have been keen on their reconciliation because in Mallika he saw an ally for more important issues. Apparently Mallika and Pasenadi never quarrelled again. Instead, as pleasant companions they often sat on the upper storey of the palace to discuss philosophical questions, seeking the Buddha's advice when they struck an impasse. Once, the king asked Mallika whether one's ego was dearest to oneself. Here the Pali word used was *attā* – the equivalent of *atman* in Sanskrit – a Brahmanical concept concerning the eternal ego of the universe and of every individual. Both felt their ego was dearest to them, but they sensed that self-love went against the universal love preached by the Buddha. So they went to Jetavana, where the Buddha agreed that one's ego was dearest to oneself, but that such self-love should not prove injurious to others.[37] Here we see the Buddha facing an audience that was also receptive to Brahmanical teachings, and tactfully resolving differences in the approach of the two doctrines.

The Buddha did not, however, compromise on the major ethical issues, or on religious practices that had a negative social impact, such as the Brahmanical practice of sacrificing cows and sheep to

---

[36] *Sujata Jataka*, no. 306 in *Jataka Stories*, pp. 13–14.
[37] *Sanyutta Nikaya*, III.i.8, pt 1, pp. 101–2, *Udana* V, 1, pt II, p. 56.

please their gods. Pasenadi, like the other kings of his time, employed Brahmans to strategise on military and state affairs and communicate with the gods. Such sacrificial rites were a legacy from Vedic times, possibly a consequence of surplus livestock that needed to be culled. By the time of the Buddha the major source of wealth was rice cultivation; draft animals such as cows and buffaloes were essential for working the fields, but their numbers had declined. Increases in agricultural landholdings had reduced sheep pastures and sheep. The Buddha never denied the existence of the gods and their superiority over human beings, but he was firm in his condemnation of animal sacrifice at a time when sacrificial animals may have been both more scarce and more expensive. In this fight, the Buddha had an ally in Mallika. The story goes that once when Pasenadi heard cries in the night and could not sleep, his Brahman priests convinced him that these were the cries of former princes who had committed adultery and been condemned to suffering in hell. The remedy, they said, was to sacrifice many animals to the gods. Preparations for the sacrifice rituals alarmed Mallika, who persuaded the king to first consult the Buddha, and the sage offered a counter-explanation to the Brahman view. He said the cries were indeed from those condemned to hell who could utter no words that made sense, but that their cries had nothing to do with the king and that the sole purpose of killing animals was to earn a livelihood for Brahmans.[38] It seems Pasenadi heeded the Buddha's interpretation and the animals were not slaughtered.

The thwarted Brahmans were not so easily deterred. Because Pasenadi had other nightmares in which livestock and crops were imperilled by disasters, the king was predisposed towards sacrificial rituals. Mallika was, in many such instances, at hand to bring the Buddha into the scene, and the sage was able to explain away sixteen dreams with persuasive rationality, demonstrating they were not omens of impending calamity.[39]

[38] *Lohakumbhi Jataka*, no. 314, *Jataka Stories*, vol. VI, pp. 29–30.
[39] *Mahasupina Jataka*, no. 77, *Jataka Stories*, vol. I, pp. 187–94.

Mallika unfortunately passed away at an early age. News of her passing reached the king when he was in audience with the Buddha. Seeing the king disconsolate, the Buddha consoled him with wise thoughts on the transient nature of all life.[40]

Mallika was fortunate in that she did not live long enough to see the political turmoil that ensued when Vidudabha assassinated his father and vanquished the Sakyas. Nor did she suffer the fate of a barren queen when the son of another queen wrested power from her husband.

Samavati, Queen of Kosambi

Two women named Sama joined the bhikkhuni community near the city of Kosambi; both gave their reason for leaving home as their grief over the death of their dear friend Samavati.[41] One was from a setthi family, the other from a gahapati's. Who was this Samavati whose death had so profoundly shaken the two sisters?

This Samavati was also the daughter of an eminent setthi in Kosambi who had married Udena, king of Kosambi. In his court was another consort of the king, Magandiya, from an outstanding Brahman family called Kuru.[42] Once, Samavati noticed that her maidservant, whom she had sent out to buy flowers, started bringing back more and more flowers every morning. This maid had also taken to keeping some money for herself instead of spending it on flowers for the queen. However, when this maid heard the Buddha's preaching, she wanted to turn over a new leaf and become a virtuous person.

Samavati, discovering the reason for the maid's conversion, continued sending her to listen to the Buddha and report back on his teachings. Their conjoint devotion to the Buddha annoyed Magandiya, who hated the Buddha because her family had once

---

[40] *Anguttara-Nikāya*, V, v, 49.

[41] Psalms xxvii, xxix, *Therīgāthā*, pp. 32–3, 34–5.

[42] This story is recorded in the *Dhammapada Commentary*, quoted in Horner, *Women under Primitive Buddhism*, p. 32; *The Dhammapada*, p. 123.

offered her hand to the young Gotama but been refused. Magandiya was, it seems, a Brahman woman competing with a queen for the favour of the king. She is reported to have set fire to the house in which Samavati dwelt, burning to death both the queen and her maid. Udena, the king, eventually discovered the truth about the evil Magandiya and put her to death.

What happened to the two Samas who were Samavati's close friends? They were very likely young women in the retinue of Samavati who had followed her to the Kosambi court. Sama was in all likelihood the name they took as a sign of their devotion to their mistress. With her death, they had nowhere to go; the sangha was the obvious refuge.

This tale of Samavati and the two Samas suggests that the losers in court politics within the new states found succour with the Buddha and his sangha. The Buddhists often claimed that they converted kings, but the truth is that most kings patronised both Buddhists and various other religious sects, including Brahmans who invoked the gods to protect regimes by sacrificing animals and performing rituals. The Buddha is really the Supreme Mediator: he intervenes in and defuses tensions in the political sphere, and thus ends up harbouring and providing solace to those who have fallen.

7

Patacara and Refugees Who Fled from Cities

LIFE IN THE URBAN societies of ancient times laid bare many social maladies and human weaknesses. Among all the philosopher-preacher-meliorists of those bygone days, the Buddha seems the most motivated by compassion, the saint who offers the most promising practical guidance that will support lay followers through the difficulties of their daily life. The Buddha advised rajas in ganasanghas and kingdoms when they sought his opinion, but he was perfectly aware that they were not his most loyal listeners. Only the menace of bad karma could have prompted Ajatasattu to confess his guilt over patricide to the Buddha. Even so, the Buddha could not stop Ajatasattu conquering the Vajji. All that he could do to alleviate the suffering caused by warfare was take in refugees who had lost all means of livelihood and were willing to join the sangha.

Setthis and gahapatis were the new urban elite and were often supporters of the Buddha as generous donors. The Buddha appreciated their support and praised the way them for their ways of making a living and thereby creating social prosperity:

> Whoso is virtuous and intelligent,
> Shines like a fire that blazes [on the hill].
> To him massing wealth, like a roving bee
> Its honey gathering [and hurting naught],
> Riches mount up as ant-heaps growing high.
> When the good layman wealth has so amassed
> Able is he to benefit his clan.[1]

[1] *Dīgha Nikāya*, iii. 188, pp. 179–80.

For setthis and gahapatis, supporting the Buddhist sangha assured them of their high status in urban society. Simultaneously, even patrons as affluent as Anathapindika and Visakha needed guidance and spiritual support when they faced difficulties in either business ventures or daily life, especially with the approach of death. Not that this meant that setthis and gahapatis were in general happy to renounce worldly wealth to join the sangha. Women in households with a seemingly comfortable life joined the Buddhist sangha for their own various reasons.

Pajapati and Khema recruited quite a few women into the sangha from the new urban social elites. These were women drawn from the ranks of gahapatis and setthis, people we have seen as the financial pillars of the urban economy. Setthi is the superlative form of good (*sri*), and these were the leading figures among the gahapatis – entrepreneurs dealing in local and long-distance trade and manufacture. Setthis also controlled most of the financial resources and have been called the bankers of ancient India. State financial institutions were a thing of the future, so kings and ganasanghas all relied on setthis for support in relation to civil construction and warfare. However, while setthis were important within society, Brahmans did not normally intermarry with them, seeing them as lower in the caste hierarchy. Daughters from setthi families were more happily received in marriage by kings and nobles wishing to enhance their family interests. We also find that many such women, born in setthi families or married into them, ended up in the Buddhist sangha. Among the more than seventy bhikkhunis who left verses, thirteen were from outstanding commercial and financial families.[2]

Dhammadinna was the daughter of a gahapati and was married to a setthi of Rajagaha. Her husband Visakha left her on the pretence that he had converted to Buddhism and had thus lost interest in women. Dhammadinna decided to join the sangha instead of going back to her natal home, so Visakha "sent her to the Bhikkhunis

---

[2] Horner, *Women Under Primitive Buddhism*, p. 167.

in a golden Palanquin."³ After long and solitary meditation, Dhammadinna gained a comprehensive understanding of the Buddha's core doctrine of the Four Noble Truths and the Eight Righteous Paths. Her former husband Visakha, though himself a layman, was eager to test her knowledge. In front of the Buddha, he challenged Dhammadinna with numerous questions about the doctrine, and Dhammadinna answered them eloquently – until Visakha raised an obscure question: "And, what, lady, is the counterpart of nibbana [nirvana]?" Dhammadinna replied thus: "This question goes too far, friend Visakha, it is beyond the compass of an answer. Friend Visakha, Brahma-faring is for emergence in nibbana, for going beyond nibbana, for culminating in nibbana. Friend Visakha, if you so desire, draw near the Lord, ask him about this matter. As the Lord explains, so will you remember."⁴

The Buddha agreed with Dhammadinna on all her answers and told Visakha to remember what she had said. Dhammadinna clearly had the upper hand in the dialogue between "friends" (no longer husband and wife). In this story, Visakha's reason for sending Dhammadinna to the sangha is suspect, for Visakha himself had long been a lay patron of the Buddha and probably a financial supporter of the sangha on account of his wealth. However, he did not anticipate that the release of his wife from his household would provide her an opportunity for intellectual development far beyond his own. This dialogue between the two became a standard teaching text in the Buddhist sangha and was included in their canon. Meanwhile, Dhammadinna became an active bhikkhuni spreading Buddhist knowledge to other bhikkhunis.

Wealthy households of the day seem to have bred some free-spirited young women who broke social restraints in pursuit of their own happiness. However, sometimes misfortune befell such women and they found themselves unable to return home even if their parents were happy to have them back. It was commonplace for parents to be socially condemned if they retained their girls at home

---

³ *Therīgāthā*, commentary on psalm xii, pp. 16–17.
⁴ *Majjhima Nikaya*, I.298–305, pp. 360–7.

after puberty. Therefore such young women more often than not ended up in the Buddhist sangha.

Bhadda was one such. She was born in a setthi family and her father was the treasurer of the king of Magadha – the chief setthi of the country. Bhadda, spoilt and knowing nothing of the real world, fell in love with a robber who was taken by the king's men to be executed. Bhadda swore she would die without him. Her father, fearing for his daughter, bribed the guards, who let the man meet Bhadda while the father decked up his girl in all kinds of jewels. The robber, more interested in the jewellery than in the girl, invented an elaborate lie saying he wanted to make an offering at the mountain cliff where he was supposed to be executed. With the intervention of the mountain gods, he said, he would be given exemption from death. In this way he tricked her to the mountain precipice with the intention of pushing her over after depriving her of all her jewellery. But Bhadda saw through his plot to kill her and pushed him down the cliff instead. This made her legendary, and it was said the deity in the mountain who witnessed her feat had this to say:

> Not in every case is Man the wiser ever;
> Woman, too, when swift to see, may prove as clever.
> Not in every case is Man the wiser reckoned;
> Woman, too, is clever, and she thinks [in] but a second.[5]

Bhadda did not feel able to return home and so became a wanderer in the order of the Niganthas, i.e. the Jainas who followed Mahavira. She learned Jaina doctrine and became a famous debater. Wherever she went, she created a heap of sand and atop it set up the branch of a rose-apple tree, inviting debate. Anyone trampling the rose-apple branch could join her in debate. Bhadda was invincible until the day she encountered Sariputta, the Buddha's famous disciple. Acknowledging defeat, she then joined the Buddhist sangha and was transformed from a "hairless, dirt-laden and half-clad" ascetic into a robed bhikkhuni.[6] The change made by Bhadda

[5] *Therīgāthā,* commentary and psalm xlvi, p. 65.
[6] Ibid., pp. 63–8.

from Jainism to Buddhism indicated her transformation from an unkempt person into one who had switched to a healthy life in the sangha.

Patacara, the daughter of a setthi in Savatthi, also suffered treachery before she was adopted by the sangha. She had eloped with a servant of her household and dwelt in a hamlet. When pregnant, she wanted to return home for her confinement. Her husband, unwilling to face punishment for eloping with her, was reluctant to let her go back. She nevertheless headed home but on her way gave birth to her child on the roadside, and soon her husband caught up with her. They then continued to live in their rudimentary dwelling until she gave birth to a second child. The same night, a storm tore through their area and they were drenched by heavy rain. Her husband went off to the forest for wood with which to repair their hut, but bitten by a snake he died there. Patacara went to look for her husband at dawn, holding her two babies. Stricken by the death of her husband, she saw that rain had flooded the road. Juggling her two babies, she was crossing the flood when a hawk snatched away one of the infants, and then she lost the second when trying in vain to get the hawk to drop the first. Having now lost everything, she headed back towards her home in Savatthi, but there learned that her entire family had perished in a storm.

Having by now lost her mind as well, she wailed and wandered naked. Appearing within sight of the Buddha, the bhikkhus and bhikkhunis around him tried to prevent her coming close. But the Buddha said to her: "Sister, recover your presence of mind."[7] She gained consciousness, and embarrassed by her nudity, fell crouching on the earth in front of the Buddha. Receiving a robe thrown to her by someone in the retinue of the Buddha, she was soon dressed. The Buddha then had the decently dressed and sane Patacara admitted to the sangha. The scene of Patacara crouching in adoration of the Buddha became legendary in Buddhist art; it

---

[7] Ibid., psalm xlvii, pp. 68–73.

is likely that a beautifully executed relief on the stupa of Amaravati is a depiction of the scene (Fig. 9).

The Buddhist sangha embraced women from both elite and common families. It took in those who had lost their identities or those who had never had much of an identity because they had been abandoned by single mothers or prostitute mothers. It accepted those from outcaste communities and those who lived in forests, marshlands, and mountains; and also those who hunted and fished and spoke languages incomprehensible to Indo-European speakers. Whether of high or low family background, these were all women made miserable by the vicissitudes of life, or who had encountered problems that had made orthodox Brahmanical society cast them out. Patacara, it was said, accepted into the sangha's fold 500 mothers grieving the loss of a child. Their admission helped them overcome the loss and saved some from homelessness, or from condemnation as barren.[8] The number 500 is of course a

Fig. 9: Women worshipping the Buddha, Amaravati Stupa, Madras Museum, photo by Xinru Liu.

[9] Ibid., psalm L, pp. 77–9.

trope, but it does indicate the extent and variety of the difficulties facing women.

Isidasi was a fair-skinned girl born in Patna in a decent family. She left a long poem describing her path to the Buddhist sangha. Her loving father had tried to get her married once she came of age. However, her in-laws sent her back home because her husband was not happy living with her. Her father then tried several times to get her a groom who could live in their household, but not even beggars could be tempted to stay. Isidasi grew so desperate that she was ready to die, but then a bhikkhuni named Jinadata came to her door for alms. Serving this sister food, Isidasi realised she could join the sangha, cast off her misery, and end the dilemma she had caused her family to confront.[9] From her narrative one may surmise that she suffered from some bodily deformity which had impeded her performing the roles laid down for all women – to be a wife and a mother. Despite her affectionate parents, the sangha was her only refuge.

Dhammadinna, Bhadda, Patacara, Isidasi, and the two women named Sama we met earlier – who had joined the sangha after the demise of Queen Samavati of Kosambi – were all drawn from the urban elites of the day. Their early lives had not been spent in poverty.[10] Yet they had all suffered as a consequence of social ills in a patriarchal society that could not be remedied. They started either as domiciled daughters and wives (Dhammadinna and Isidasi), or as rebellious girls (Bhadda and Patacara), all expecting to live happy lives. They had all to take resort to both the spiritual refuge of the Buddha's teaching and the material refuge of the sangha.

Over the seventy years of his life the Buddha witnessed and was unusually sensitive to the fact of human suffering, and despite his initial reluctance to induct them into the sangha, it probably became an imperative for him to make room for women on account of the sheer scale of their suffering within a society so overwhelmingly centred on the happiness of men. His refuge for women had to be built from scratch under the supervision of Maha Pajapati.

---

[9] Ibid., psalm lxxii, pp. 156–63.
[10] *Therīgāthā*, psalms xxvii, xxix, pp. 32–3, 34–5.

As we know, the Buddhist sangha of this period had no permanent residences, so that bhikkhus and bhikkhunis wandered from town to town for daily alms and spread their leader's teachings. Rajas and setthis and gahapatis fed them and housed them. But an itinerant life made women especially vulnerable, with young and nubile bhikkhunis highly liable to sexual attack. Subba, a young bhikkhuni with beautiful eyes, when taking a nap on a hot afternoon in Jivaka's mango grove, was harassed by a young man of Rajagaha. Her anger at the lout was so extreme that she extracted one of her own eyes and handed it over to him to thwart his desire. A long poem, supposedly composed by Subba herself, tells this story; luckily it ends happily, with the Buddha miraculously restoring her sight – using the power derived from her own accumulation of merit.[11]

Women who had experienced traumas and joined the sangha seemed to have found a clean and healthy environment, even if a fixed residence was lacking. The availability of a sisterhood provided them with, at the very least, a space for recovery and reflection and perhaps reconciliation with the world they had no option but to live in. The major disciplinary rules of monastic life were probably already in place when Maha Pajapati began recruiting female novices. What made the Buddhist sangha different from other religious communities – and even from the Jain communities which shared similar views of the world – was the Buddha's insistence that his followers pay attention to personal hygiene and be modest in their dress.

There was, additionally, the pivotal figure of Jivaka, who had helped establish health as an aspect of Buddhist discipline at a time when the sangha was expanding rapidly, absorbing within its fold political losers and the socially disadvantaged. The Buddha had already ruled that those in the sangha should not be naked.[12] However, he did not have the resources to clothe his followers decently, and not even himself, so that bhikkhus picked up rags from trash heaps or cemeteries to cover themselves. Subsequently,

[11] Ibid., psalm lxxi, pp. 148–55.
[12] *Vinaya Texts*, Cullavagga, V.15.1, p. 110.

as noted, it was Jivaka who convinced the Buddha that brothers in the sangha should accept clean clothes as donations from their lay followers.[13] He also advised the Buddha on the sangha's need for sanitation and for personal hygiene among his followers, and regular bathing in established facilities was made a norm.[14] In time the sangha also established an office for distributing clothing received as gifts to monks, and laid down a dress code.[15] This clothing code was in place when Pajapati pleaded to the Buddha to let Sakya women join the sangha – she herself had donned an orange robe when starting on her trip to Vesali.[16] Overall, these hygiene and clothing rules are likely to have been strong incentives for women to seek out the sangha.

A set of rules more specifically in relation to bhikkhunis gradually took shape. Women from various backgrounds having joined the sangha, special rules were needed to set their lives straight and be made uniform. Khema came in from royalty, Patacara was totally distraught. Others came in pregnant, and the prospect of infants within the sangha then required rules helping mothers to raise their children. One of the rules, in keeping with the idea of austerity and simplicity, stipulated that women of the sangha not wear luxurious dresses or use cosmetics, regardless of how accustomed they may have been to such things in their earlier secular lives.[17] A second rule forbade the use of intoxicating substances, regardless of the woman's level of distress: we have earlier noted the arrival of the word asava, which appears frequently in Pali texts and indicates a new phenomenon at the time of the Buddha. In Vedic sacrificial ceremonies, soma, an intoxicant, stimulates priests to connect with gods; by contrast the Buddha's belief in disciplined meditation was to rid people of maya, a condition induced by hallucinations.

[13] *Vinaya Texts*, Mahāvagga, VIII,1.30–5, pp. 191–5.
[14] Ibid., 14, pp. 103–10.
[15] Ibid. The entire chapter of Mahāvagga VIII is about establishing the dress code of the sangha: pp. 171–255.
[16] *Vinaya Texts*, Cullavagga, X.I, 2, p. 321.
[17] Ibid., X. 10, 1, pp. 340–1.

We have discussed asava earlier; however, the word needs further discussion here because it had a particular relevance to bhikkhunis. The Buddha gave an entire discourse on the problems of asava under the title *Sabbāsavasutta*, meaning "discourse of all *asavas*".[18] Later, in the *Arthashastra* of Sanskrit literature (three centuries or more later), asava designates a kind of potent alcohol.[19] Alcohol addiction could well have been a common phenomenon in the new cities which were dotted with taverns, and the Buddha was certainly worried enough about alcohol addiction to set down specific rules on drink. In his list of permitted drinks are many kinds of juices made from South Asian fruits, such as the mango, grape, plantain, the root of the water lily, and sugarcane. Rules about juices from leaves and flowers are more nuanced because they were more likely to produce suspicious substances.[20] These worries are echoed in the psalms composed by bhikkhunis, which include the declaration that they must finally get rid of all asavas.[21] Bhikkhunis were, after all, more vulnerable to being preyed upon if intoxicated, and it seemed to them imperative to be rid of substances that had induced them, or could induce them again, into wretchedness. From the psalms some of these women wrote, it is evident that for them the Buddhist sangha was not merely an asylum but also an educational institution where they could reconstitute their identity and their life. At a time when education was still very much the monopoly of Brahman men, these sisters in the Buddhist sangha expressed their life stories and thoughts, their joys and sorrows, their fears and their hopes, in beautiful poems which offer us at least a hazy picture of the lives they led.

---

[18] *Majjhima Nikaya*, I.6–12, pp. 8–16.
[19] *Kautiliya Arthasastra*, 2.25.7.
[20] *Vinaya Texts*, Mahāvagga, VI, 35, 6, pp. 132–3.
[21] For example, IV Tissā, pp. 12–13; XXXVIII, an anonymous sister, pp. 50–1; XXXIX, Vimalā, pp. 52–3; etc.

8
Newcomers from Forests, Mountains, and Waters

MANY OF THE WOMEN who lived in the new cities at the time of the Buddha could not trace their birth to Vedic lineages – neither to the solar line nor to the lunar line, be they queens such as Mallika or daughters and wives from elite families such as Patacara. Many of them had no family to claim at all, such as Ambapali in Vesali and Salavati in Rajagaha. Kings, gahapatis, and setthis too were not from the Vedic lineages, so that they made marriage arrangements for political connections and economic networks, and then created pseudo-exalted family lineages and affiliations for themselves. But where were the women who claimed no birthplace and family in cities originally from?

Outside, around the cities, were cultivated lands and pastoral patches dotted by villages. Here, most residents were peasant farmers who were either Sudras or other low castes, or outcastes. These were low-status people who belonged nonetheless to the Brahmanical ethos and cultural domain, and who shared the same languages and religious concepts as the urbanites.

Further from the cities and along routes linking the cities lived people who were either exiled from mainstream society or were the original inhabitants of mountains, forests, and marshlands. Because such folk did not share the languages and values of the new state culture, their ways of life and genealogies were irrelevant to the urban population as well as to villagers. Such people did nevertheless have contact and interchanges with saints and ascetics of the various religious sects who had chosen to leave the noise of the cities and dwell with their thoughts and practices in forests. Conversely, hunters and fishermen had heard of the fantastic lives possible in cities and sought opportunities there, though they were looked down upon by suspicious city dwellers. Meanwhile, the communities they came from were made up of those who worshipped nagas (snakes or "dragons"), trees, and spirits. Their habitations were not all that far from the outskirts of the cities. Those who did not migrate into the cities to work sometimes took to highway robbery and pillage on routes cutting through the forests, mountains, and waters that linked the cities. Their domain, with its own norms and rules, was a counterpoint to the dominant cultural world of the states built by the Indo-European-speaking communities which had spread on the Indus-Gangetic plain by the time of the Buddha. These people who lived at various edges and inside notches outside the urban domain injected fresh energy and talent into the urban centres. Cities of that period, as well as of the ensuing 2000 years, were seldom free of disease or unthreatened by warfare; the always dwindling urban population was thus continually in need of replenishment from the world beyond it. Forest and marshland dwellers not only served this purpose but were providers of iron ore, minerals, elephants, beasts of burden, meat, fish, and other water products.

In their horse sacrifice ceremonies, Brahman priests are seen addressing spirits unknown in the *Rg Veda*, such as female celestial beings called apsaras and male ones called gandharvas — all musicians and dancers.[1] There were also some less beautiful beings they needed to deal with, such as the king of the snakes who headed the many snake cults that had spread across India; and then there was Kubera Vaisravana, the god who commanded many nasty beings such as rakshasas, villains, and robbers (*papakrita, selaga*).[2] Though these various spirits received different levels of respect in the Brahman

---

[1] *Satapata Brahmana*, XIII 4.4.7–8, pp. 365–6.
[2] Ibid., 4.4.9–10, pp. 367–8.

ceremonies, they were all part of the pantheon. Kubera became a popular deity among many religious sects where he was known as the commander of the Yakshas (Yakkhas in Pali). Yakshas appear vaguely in the *Ṛg Veda* but later grow into a great variety of creatures in human form, male and female. Some of them can be attractive or beautiful, whereas others are bloodthirsty and ugly robbers and thugs – and all come under the command of Kubera.

During the middle of the first millennium BCE the Buddha and other thinkers were face to face with this panorama of religious devotion for deities ranging from the Vedic tradition to the various cults worshipped by those coming into villages and cities, or who continued in forests and marshlands. Cults of Yakshas, Nagas, Apsaras, and Gandharvas permeated the territory and infiltrated all new schools of faith. Religious sects recruited members from these cults and many who joined a new order continued with their adherence to the traditional deities they and their community had long worshipped. The theologians of Jainism, Brahmanism, and Buddhism all tried to reconceptualise the great variety of spirits, to accommodate and integrate them into some kind of syncretic framework which would still remain distinctively theirs. They usually ended up creating varying divine and human hierarchies in line with their own perspective of the universe.[3] Early Buddhists, for example, abhorred the use of alcohol and blood sacrifice in Yaksha and Naga and other cults but did not condemn the followers of these cults as incurable scoundrels.[4]

By the third century BCE, when Ashoka consolidated most parts of the subcontinent under the Mauryan Empire, the Buddhist sangha faced a crisis with the splitting of the institution by a sectarian interpretation of the doctrine. Without the leadership of the Buddha himself, Ashoka had to interfere by issuing an edict to expel dissident monks and make them wear a white robe.[5] At the same time, the dichotomy between state societies

---

[3] Decaroli, *Haunting the Buddha*, pp. 10ff.
[4] Ibid., pp. 24–5.
[5] Thapar, *Cultural Pasts*, p. 224.

and "outsiders" came to be more clearly marked. In his famous Thirteenth Edict in the aftermath of the Kalinga war, Ashoka categorised his subjects as "Brahmana, Shramana, and all sects [*prashamda* or *pasamda*], and householders." Even the Greeks, whom he called Yona, were within the fold of law-abiding subjects of his empire, though their religion was quite different from the Buddhism he favoured, and from Brahmanism and any other sects that had originated in India. Even those who lived in the forests, the Atavi – who were not adherents of any of the recognised religions but of cults worshipping deities in the shape of snakes, half-humans, or grotesque forms – were sought to be assured by Ashoka's decision to let everyone live in peace so long as they made no trouble for settled people.[6]

In the three hundred and more years of state development, urbanisation, and social change that separated the Buddha and his sangha from Ashoka, a variety of Brahman rishis, Jainas, Buddhists, and other dissident religious communities constituted the link between settled civilisation and those who were nomadic or itinerant or resident outside cities. The settlement of Buddhists and other organised religions within deep forests was invariably aimed at introducing Buddhist religious practice to these outsiders, but meanwhile brought folk cults into the settled world.

In much of the early religious literature, women from obscure backgrounds, as noted, feature as the consorts or mothers of major heroes in state-creation legends: Shakuntala (the mother of Bharata), and Sakuntala (the faggot gatherer of the jatakas) being archetypical. As these legendary mothers of heroes could not have come out of nowhere, they were very likely the legacy of intermarriages between Vedic lineages (in theory patriarchal) and indigenous matrilineal communities. These matrilineal communities continued to exist outside urban-rural settlements in the time of the Buddha. The legacy of many of the Buddha's disciples was from communities in which the mother's status was higher than the

---

[6] The two passages appear in several versions of the Major Rock Inscriptions of Ashoka XIII: Hultzsch, *Inscriptions of Asoka*.

father's: Sariputta and Moggallana, we have seen, used their mothers' names. Sariputta was the son of Rupasari, and Moggallana was the son of Moggali.[7] Close bonds between mothers and sons constituted a common phenomenon among the Buddha's followers. Rather than male ancestor worship, Buddhists were more concerned with the well-being of deceased mothers.

Women therefore also feature considerably in the Buddhist literature and the earliest artworks that Buddhists carved on monuments. They are manifest in Buddhist stories and carvings partly to propagate the new faith to those likely to be predisposed to conversion on account of their existence within a matrilineal culture.

Sculptural art flourished in the Mauryan Empire, especially during the reign of Ashoka. The stupas at Sanchi in Central India were built at this time, probably with the emperor's patronage, suggested by the existence of a pillar carved with one of his edicts which stood just beside the major stupa. The message in the edict includes this:

> The [split-up] sangha, both of monks and of nuns, has been made one united whole. As long as [my] sons and great-grandsons [shall rule] and the moon and sun [shall shine], monks or nuns who create a division in the sangha shall be made to put on white robes and to reside out of the [sangha] . . . For what is my desire? – That the sangha as a united [body] may long endure.[8]

From the arrangement of the stupa and the edict pillar, it seems possible that Ashoka had the monument built to stave off a crisis of division within the sangha – because he trusted the sangha there to carry out his mission of pacifying the tribes of the forest. The Sanchi monastic complex lay deep in a forest, along one of the routes connecting the Ganges plain from Kosambi to the ports of the west coastal region. Even then, some three hundred or more years after the Buddha, the stupa (topa in the

---

[7] *Theragatha*, CCLIX, *Sariputta* commentary, pp. 340–1.
[8] Marshall, *et al.*, *The Monuments of Sanchi*, vol. I, p. 287.

vernacular) was a bare dome containing relics of the Buddha. Even after the Mauryan Empire declined, images of the Buddha himself were still absent. What continued, however, were numerous sculptures showing a variety of cults – awe-striking Nagas, beautiful Yakkhis, ghost-like human figures, and many kinds of kinnara (half-human, half-animal creatures). Such sculptures and reliefs were executed through donations by people whose names included references to Nagas, Yakkhas, and Bhutas. In other words, the donors were from communities worshipping cults of these names.

The relief panels on the southern gate's arch of Stupa 1 – the main entrance accessing the dome – depict scenes of Ashoka's patronage and jataka stories. On the middle crossbar of the arch, the most eminent place for a visual message, is a scene of Ashoka riding on a royal chariot approaching a stupa from the left side, followed by a large retinue of horse riders, elephant riders, and pedestrians, with winged creatures hovering above. On the other side of the central stupa is a Naga king wearing a hood of five cobra heads and surrounded by a retinue of men and women wearing the hoods of one or more cobras. The Naga king is also protected by winged kinnaras. Several smaller panels on the pillar of the arch depict Ashoka's visits to the Bodhi tree and stupas in a more ordinary way. A relief showing a grieving Ashoka worshipping a lock of the Buddha's hair is signed by a guild of ivory carvers from the city of Vedisa, capital of the Sunga Dynasty, which succeeded the Mauryan Empire in the Greater Magadha region.[9]

The Sunga Dynasty claimed a Brahman lineage and built its new capital Vedisa at a distance from the Mauryan Pataliputra. The memory of Ashoka persisted, however, in the former frontier but also now in the metropolis of the new regime, as shown in signed work by ivory artists and many donors from the city of Vedisa in the environs of the Sanchi Stupa.

Nagas appeared on Buddhist monuments as cobras as well as

---

[9] Ibid. p. 342, no. 400; American Institute of Indian Studies, neg. no. 320.95.

human figures wearing the hoods of cobras. When human settlements encroached the wild lands, they inevitably ran into snakes, with cobras plentiful and much feared for their power to inflict a swift death, which then meant a perspective from which they were seen as the weapons of a deity, or as deities themselves. The Buddha told his bhikkhus not to kill nagas: "Let the cobra be, do not touch the cobra, do reverence to the cobra." He even described his disciples Moggallana and Sariputta as "Mahanaga" – an image of the incorruptible monk.[10] With the proliferation of cobra cults, communities that took on this form of worship called themselves Nagas. When the Buddha speaks of respecting the cobra, what he means is that Buddhists need to get along with the Naga cults. The chiefs showing cobra hoods in the Sanchi panels alongside a royal figure are very possibly representations of the chiefs of Naga communities.

Among the several "Nagarajas" who helped the cause of the Buddha, Mucalinda, who had a legend woven around him, is probably the one who has lasted the longest. It started with the young Sakyamuni in his early days as an ascetic dwelling in Uruvela village (later Bodh Gaya). The story goes that, when seated in a single posture for seven days in rainy weather, "Mucalinda, the snake rajah, coming forth from [a] hunt, encircled the body of the Exalted One seven times with his coils and stood rearing his great hood above the Exalted One's head: yet not heat or cold or the touch of flies, mosquitoes, wind and heat or creeping things annoyed the Exalted One."[11] A Sanchi railing pillar depicts this story, though the Buddha is shown not in his human form but as the flame in the altar at the centre (see Fig. 1). We are also told that when the sky cleared, the young Sakyamuni awoke from deep thought and saw a young man standing in front of him, his hands folded reverentially.[12]

---

[10] *Majjhima Nikaya*, I.32, 146, pp. 40, 186.
[11] *Udāna*, II.I, p. 12.
[12] Ibid., p. 13.

Numerous reliefs and sculptures on the arches and railings around the barren dome of the Sanchi Stupa show scenes of mystics living a forest life with all kinds of trees, plants, animals, Nagas, and Yakkhas. Sculptures of Yakkhis hanging on tree branches function as brackets supporting the structure of the northern and eastern arches and are the overwhelmingly artistic feature of the entire architecture. Ugly dwarf Yakkhas carry the burden of the western arch.[13] Though no names are carved on the statues to identify the cults they represent, donors who had the artworks done left names associated with specific cults, cities, and professions.

Women, in general, show a strong presence among the more than 800 donors who recorded their names in the period before the coming of the Kushans at the start of the Christian era. These are wives, mothers, nuns, and lay followers of the Buddha. A woman named Naga is the wife of a setthi from a place called Kamdadigama, or the village of Kamdadi;[14] a bhikkhuni called Yakkhi is from the city of Vedisa;[15] another Naga is a lay follower who has made two donations from a place called Tiridapada, or the tribe of Tirida. A bhikkhuni with the name Yakhadasi, meaning the slave of Yakkha or Yakkha's slave, indicates she was, at least at some point, or when she made the donation honouring the Buddha, a follower of the Yakkha cult.[16] A woman called Vakala Devi identifies herself as the mother of her son, Ahimitra.[17] If this Vakala was a queen, as the title Devi indicates, she may have been the chief of a small matrilineal regime. The evidence certainly suggests that women were dominant among the new supporters of Buddhism, and that a number of them were drawn to the sangha from circumambient cults.

The colourful universe on the Sanchi Stupa and the diverse types of donors it contains suggest a land full of Nagas paying obeisance

[13] Marshall, *et al.*, *The Monuments of Sanchi*, vol. II.
[14] Ibid., no. 42, p. 303.
[15] Ibid., no. 137, p. 313.
[16] Ibid., no. 326, p. 332.
[17] Ibid., no. 364, p. 337.

to the Buddha and in contact with happenings in the mainstream of the new states. A regime of cobra-worshipping Nagas became regents of the land under the Sunga regime.[18] The picture we have here is of communities of Naga worshippers who continue as cult worshippers while deferring to the Buddha: the probable trajectory, a couple of centuries into the Christian era, results in the Buddhist philosophers Nagarjuna, as well as the sage Nagasena.

The Bharhut Stupa, also in the orbit of the Nagas to the north of Sanchi, suggests the story of native cults assimilated into the Buddhist universe in a slightly different way. The initial construction of the Bharhut Stupa dates to later than Sanchi in the Sunga period. Ashoka is not obviously present in the scenes here. Royal patronage of the huge work involved came from a minor royal called Dhanabhuti, who was followed by his son and a female royal called Nagarakhita, meaning "protected by the Naga".[19] This minor royal family acknowledged the suzerainty of the Sungas. As in Sanchi, women made donations here out of their own coffers. Of the 136 donors recorded, 58 were laymen and 36 laywomen; from among members of the sangha, 25 bhikkhus made donations, as did 16 bhikkhunis.[20] Many of the names of donors, men and women, are associated with Nagas, Bhutas, Yakkhas, and Yakkhis. Some of the donors indicated an association with the Vedic tradition via names such as "deva", "Inda" (Indra), and "mita" (*mitra*).[21] A woman, Chapadeva, wife of Revatimita from the city of Vedisa, cuts a majestic figure holding a casket of the Buddha's relics on the main entrance of the stupa.[22] The name of the donor, Chapadeva,

[18] Joseph Schwartzberg marks the territory of the Nagas in this region (EF4 of Plate 21a): Schwartzberg, *A Historical Atlas of South Asia*.

[19] *Bharhut Inscriptions*, vol. II, A3, A4, pp. 11–15.

[20] Ibid., pp. 1–2.

[21] Ibid., Naga: A4, Nagarakhita, p. 15; A11, Nagadeva, p. 18; A24, Diganaga, p. 23; A54b, Nagarakhita, p. 35; A70, Aya Nagadeva, p. 42; A74, Nāgā Bichuni, p. 44; Bhuta: A35, Bhutarakhita p. 25; A38, Aya-Bhutarakhita, pp. 27–8; A78, Bhutā Bichhuni, p. 45; Yakha: A105, Yakhila, p. 54; A116 Yakhī, pp. 57–8; Indra: A45, Indadevā, pp. 30–1; Mitra: A121, Mitadeva, p. 59.

[22] Indian Museum, Calcutta, no. 108, courtesy American Institute of Indian Studies, neg. no. 243.40.

NEWCOMERS FROM FORESTS, MOUNTAINS   157

is clearly declared on the side of the chief royal figure near her. She seems to have been a married woman, a matriarch in an elite household. Her status and wealth gave her the right to have her name shown on the first pillar of the large railing (Fig. 10). The chief royal figure depicted is almost certainly the leader of a ceremony showing the entry of the relic casket into the stupa. He perhaps represents certain mythical royal patrons in the Buddhist memory,

Fig. 10: "Vedisa Chapadevaya Revatimita Bhariyaya pathama thabho danam", Indian Museum, Calcutta, no. 108, courtesy of the American Institute of Indian Studies at the Van Pelt Library, University of Pennsylvania, neg. no. 243.40.

or else the emperor Ashoka. Given that the Bharhut Stupa was built under the broad auspices of the Sunga regime and in the neighbourhood of the Sunga capital Vedisa, it may have seemed politic to the donor to avoid naming the king of a dynasty overthrown by the Sungas. It is however unlikely that the role of Ashoka in promoting Buddhism will have been missed by devotees, given his prominence within the tradition.

The layout of sculptures and reliefs at the Bharhut Stupa is distinct from that at the Sanchi Stupa in that human-size statues of Yakkhas, Yakkhis, and Devatas feature on the main pillars of the railings facing the bare dome at the centre. Here again, however, the Buddha appears in the form of a Bodhi tree, or as footprints, whereas the identity of the cults, such as of Kubera Yakho – the king of all Yakkhas – is clearly marked. A Yakkha called Suchiloma stands on one of the pillars in a pious pose. This Yakkha is elsewhere reported as impertinent when he first approaches the Buddha at Gaya:

> Suchiloma said: "I will ask thee a question, O Samana; if thou cannot answer it, I will either scatter thy thoughts or cleave thy heart, or take thee by the feet and throw thee over to the other shore of the Ganga."
>
> Bhagavat answered: "I do not see, O friend, neither in this world together with the world of the Devas, Maras, Brahmanas, nor amongst the generation of Samana and Brahmanas, gods and men, the one who can either scatter my thoughts or cleave my heart, or take me by the feet and throw me over to the other shores of Ganga. However ask O friend, what thou pleasest."[23]

However, the disposition of the statue of Suchiloma suggests calm, and in its stone form there is no trace of a brutal Yakkha intending harm to the Buddha (Fig. 11).

We also see a Sirima Devata here who could well represent the courtesan transformed into a goddess in Rajagaha and given entry into the Thirty-three Heavens of Sakka (Fig. 6).

---

[23] *The Sutta-Nipāta*, 5, "Sukilomasuta", pp. 44–5.

NEWCOMERS FROM FORESTS, MOUNTAINS   159

Fig. 11: Suchiloma Yakkho at the Great railing of the Bharhut Stupa, Indian Museum, Calcutta, no. 144, American Institute of Indian Studies, neg. no. 244.7.

Not all the cult figures are identifiable by inscribed names, probably on account of damage to the monuments. A woman holding a stringed instrument, probably a vina, provokes imagination of her role in the heavenly world. As a whole, the circle of large sculpted figures around the Bharhut Stupa symbolises an expansion of new deities who have joined the heavenly space of Buddhism from spaces outside the mainstream.

Meanwhile, the scene of the Thirty-three Heavens, as described in the *Vimanavatthu: Stories of the Mansions*, is carved on one of the gate pillars. Celebrating the enlightenment of the Buddha, four women dance while following an orchestra of vinas, drums, and hand-clappers.[24]

Fig. 12: Celebrating the enlightenment of the Buddha, Indian Museum, no. 182, American Institute of Indian Studies, neg. no. 484.76.

[24] *Bharhut Inscriptions*, Inscriptions B.21.22, Plates xxxvi, xviii, pp. 93–4; Indian Museum, no. 182, American Institute of Indian Studies, neg. no. 484.76.

We have earlier seen a similar troupe within another scene of heavenly celebration where the dancers wear costumes, their performance mimicking the gods (see Fig. 7).[25] Inscriptions attached to the scene provide the names of the four dancing accharas (apsaras in Sanskrit), and remarkably three of them – Alambusa, Missakesi, and Subhadda – are famed dancers in the Buddhist stories of the heavenly mansions.[26] The composition of the Bharhut Stupa, in short, is a display of cults of various traditions together performing a worship ceremony to the dome, which is a symbol of the permanent presence of the Buddha by the fact of containing his relics.

The Sanchi and Bharhut stupas both disappeared from the vision of Buddhists after about the second or third century CE, when Hellenistic, Iranian, and Central Asian artists added their memories to the artworks here. Chinese pilgrims who tracked sacred sites in India never visited these two sites. Perhaps the Buddhist institutions there collapsed with the loss of state sponsorship. The local forest communities around the stupas are unlikely to have diminished because the environment continued throwing up women who asserted their own rights and status as heads of families.

---

[25] *Bharhut Inscriptions*, Inscriptions B.27, 28, 30, 31, Plates xxxvii, xviii, 100–4; Indian Museum, no. 273, American Institute of Indian Studies, neg. no. 484.58.

[26] *Vimanavatthu*, 18.11, p. 43.

9

From Aryans to Chandalas

A Mobile Hierarchy in the Buddhist Universe

IN THE ECONOMIST Daniel Kahneman's argument, the intensity of sadness and loss is much greater than the happiness brought by gain.[1] If this is true, people even in a prosperous society feel pain more acutely than they experience joy. The Buddha seems to have sensed something like this social fact 2500 years ago. He understood that the dominant framework of his time, the Brahmanical caste system, determined how the individual, whether rich or poor, was going to be able to live his or her life. Social status, which was mostly determined at birth – with only some exceptions being able to escape its constraints and make good via the new possibilities of an urban life – was ultimately the great grid determining a person's acquisition of wealth and power. To improve matters for all and create a new framework which critiqued, contested, and invalidated the Brahmanical worldview was the only method by which generalised social, economic, and cultural change was possible. And to crack the old mould and create a new vision along which people could think differently and reconceive their personal capacities and life's possibilities meant that the Buddha had to be a moral guide who was offering, effectively and attractively, a new explanation of the universe in which all creatures might live more equally, more harmoniously, and less hierarchically than under Brahmanism.

[1] Kahneman, *Thinking, Fast and Slow*, pp. 278–99.

To this end, the sage outlined an eventual goal for every living creature which involved getting out of the many cycles of rebirth to which life forms were subject, in order to reach the state of nirvana. Beyond this, his receptivity to suggestion and opinion from those around him, such as Jivaka, represented a break from conservative Brahman orthodoxy which was suspicious of any changes that suggested an egalitarian trajectory. As against most other sects in which followers practised asceticism in dirty rags and filthy settings, Buddhist monks and nuns, though seldom in permanent residences, were enjoined clean robes, personal hygiene, and sanitary living. To outline and explain this encompassing vision of social change, the Buddha formulated a set of "noble truths" that were easy to comprehend and follow by all, and a philosophy of natural and supernatural existence that was likely to seem both plausible and consoling to his audience. The universe he postulated was constituted of several realms of creatures.

The Realm of the Devas

Numerous gods appear in the Vedas, while in the Upanisads – the later Vedic literature ascribed to named teachers – the number of gods is consolidated to thirty-three. The sage Yajnavalkya explains that the 3303 gods mentioned in rituals represent the "power of gods". There are, however, only thirty-three gods: the eight Vasus are fire, earth, the intermediate region, sun, sky, moon, and stars; the eleven Rudras are the ten functions (*prana*) in a man with the atman as the eleventh; the twelve Adityas are the twelve months of the year. Together with Indra (thunder) and Prajapati (sacrifice) there are, in sum, thirty-three gods.[2] Yajnavalkya also divides the heaven of the gods into four quarters: in the eastern quarter resides the sun; in the southern quarter lives Yama; in the western quarter there is Varuna; and the god of the northern quarter is the moon. In addition, there is the god of fire on the zenith looking over them all.[3]

[2] *Upanisads, Brhadaranyaka Upanisad*, 3.9.1–10, pp. 46–7.
[3] Ibid., 3.9.18–25, pp. 49–51.

The Upanisadic version of the heavens became the foundation for the Buddhist realm of the devas. In it, the highest realm in the universe outside the state of nirvana was the realm of the devas. This was seen as an outcome in the Brahmanical tradition of the conflict between devas and asuras. After Indra (Sakka, in Buddhist narratives) had defeated the asuras, he built a palace of victory called Vejayanta to house thirty-three devas, including himself, so that it came to be known as the heavenly palace of the Thirty-three Devas (Tāvatiṁsa in Pali). As noted earlier, in it female musicians who have acquired enough merit play instruments to entertain the devas. When Moggallana visited this heaven to check on the doings of the devas, "as a daughter-in-law shrinks and is shy on seeing her father-in-law, even so did the female attendants of Sakka, the lord of devas, seeing the venerable Moggallana the Great, shrinking and shy, each enter her own inner room." Other major figures in this palace were Vessavana, a great raja, and Kubera, chief of the Yakkhas.[4] In this heaven Sakka is not the warrior Indra of the *Ṛg Veda* but a benevolent god who, along with the chief of the Yakkhas, rules over the beautiful female musicians and Yakkhas. The early Buddhists had obviously adapted the heavens of the devas from Brahmanical traditions for their own reconceptualisation.

A scene showing the deva realm is a relief carved on a pillar of the southern gate of the Bharhut Stupa (now in the Indian Museum at Calcutta). It shows the Buddhist modification of the Upanisadic deva-heaven.[5] Inscriptions on the upper-left corner designate the eastern region of this heaven; the one on the upper-right corner shows the northern district; the lower-right represents the southern region; the inscription on the lower-left is missing but is bound to have related to the western region.[6] The gods on the panel are divided by tree branches into four sections, though there is no clear

[4] *Dīgha Nikāya*, III.202, pp. 193–4.
[5] American Institute of Indian Studies' photo archive at the library of the University of Pennsylvania, Indian Museum 272; American Institute of Indian Studies, neg. 3.23.81, courtesy of the library of the University of Pennsylvania.
[6] *Bharhut Inscriptions*, B24–26, Plates XVIII and XXXVII.

designation distinguishing the gods in each section. All the devas are good-looking and show respect to the Buddha. Only those on the lower-left section carry special features: the two on the left have cobra heads sticking out of their headgear. The god on the right of the section has two wings, symbolising perhaps his ability to fly like a bird. The character sitting in the corner of the western section of heaven could be the defeated Mara, who looks depressed because he has been beaten and awaits being driven from the realm

Fig. 13: The realm of the gods, Bharhut Stupa, Indian Museum, no. 271, American Institute of Indian Studies, neg. 23.81.

of the gods. A fat and happy figure on the upper-right corner, outside the northern district, could be Kubera, chief of all Yakkhas (Yakshas). In this version of the realm of their gods the Buddhists have added Kubera, Nagas (via the cobras), and winged gods, and very probably the defeated Mara. This scene agrees with the literature on Moggallana's visit to the heaven of the Thirty-three Devas, where both Indra and Kubera serve as his guides.

The statue of Kubera on one of the major pillars surrounding the Bharhut Stupa shows a serious worshipper of the Buddha and a cult of the Yakkhas.

Fig. 14: Kubera Yakkho, Indian Museum, no. 105, AIIs neg. # 482.89, courtesy of the Library of the University of Pennsylvania.

A large number of female artists permeate Buddhist art, all the way from the early days of Buddhism at Sanchi and Bharhut to sculptures and murals in north-west India, Afghanistan, Central Asia, and China. Nagas, Yakkhas, and courtesans seemed to have a better chance of gaining entry into the heavenly realms – excluding heaven's core – than Brahmans, gahapatis, and setthis.

The Realm of Humans

Below the heavens lives the Buddha in a world divided into communities of high and low social status. Brahmanical society, as is familiar, had four varnas: Brahman, Ksatriya, Vaisya, and Sudra. "Like lineage, varna was a mechanism for assimilation and arises with stratification but pre-dated the conditions conducive to a possible class society."[7] The assertion here is that in this framework the priests of communities joining the Brahmanical culture could become Brahmans; rulers and oligarchs could claim Ksatriya status; householders, merchants, and all those whom we call "middle class" could be Vaisyas; and peasants were definitely Sudras. Varnas were not directly correlated with economic status. At the time that state societies came into being, varna was still a valid concept that people used to label themselves and others. Varna literally means colour, and the Brahmans had assigned a symbolic colour to each group. In a late-Vedic ritual text, when deciding on the ground for situating his house, a man is advised to dig a knee-deep pit, then fill it with earth and water it. He should next examine the colour of this patch of ground. The colour white would indicate that the place is suited to a Brahman; red for a Ksatriya; and yellow for a Vaisya.[8] No colour is assigned to Sudras, perhaps because they were of such low status that they were not thought worthy of a proper house.

In real life, however, jati, or status at birth, was the word for social groups of distinguishable occupation bound by family ties.

[7] Thapar, *From Lineage to State*, p. 170.
[8] *Asvalayana, Grihya Sutra*, in the *Grihya Sutras*, II, 8.1–10, p. 212.

Developments in farming, trade, handicraft, finance, and the urban economy created numerous occupations which were grouped around familial cores. Gahapatis and setthis, for example, were the most distinguished in the cities but without a clear varna designation. Vendors and growers and makers of various products such as brassware, textiles, flowers, and ivory were organised into jatis that were similar to guilds in the Western world. Commercial transactions needed scribes to record deals; epidemic diseases called for caregivers and physicians; musicians and dancers organised themselves in matriarchal families to entertain both city dwellers and travellers to the city; butchers, and hunters who brought them meat, were considered polluting and thus of low status; and the lowest in the jati ordering were Chandalas, who cleaned out the garbage of the city but were considered so polluting that they had to live in separate settlements outside it.

Some non-Brahmanical thinkers tried to assign colours indicating status to various occupational-familial jatis. A sage named Purana Kassapa assigned six colours to hordes of jatis: black to jatis of "Mutton butchers, pork butchers, fowlers, hunters, thugs, fishermen, robbers, cut-throats, jailers and all others who follow a bloody trade." The colour blue indicated "monks who lived as though with a thorn in their side . . "; red was for Jains and folk in loincloth; yellow was for "white robed householders and followers of naked ascetics"; white was for "fakirs and their disciples"; and the purest white was for a few of the sage's favourite ascetics.[9] In this scheme of differentiation, except for the black-coloured jatis – whose occupations involved killing – all the others were ascetics of different sects.

The Buddha rejected this elaborate hierarchisation and colour labelling as foolish and lacking in common sense. His own view of vanna (varna) for all jatis was that there is only either black or white, and these two colours indicated both birth status and deeds performed in the material realm.

[9] *Anguttara-Nikāya*, VI, vi, 57, p. 273.

> One reborn in a low-caste clan – pariah, hunter, weaver, wheelwright, sweeper – in a poor family, where food and drink are scarce, life is hard, keep and clothing [are difficult to] come by; and he is ugly, ill-featured, misshapen and much afflicted, being blind, deformed in the hand, lame or crippled, and is no recipient of food, drink, clothes, carriage, flowers, scents, ointments, bed, lodging or lighting [is black by birth].

If he then follows the wrong path in the course of his life, he will go to hell after death, for his dhamma – shown by his activity – is also black. A black birth is thus the outcome of a combination of bad occupation, poverty, and misfortunes such as are caused by disease. Yet all who may have begun life with a black birth could aspire to and actually reach the heavens if they followed the right path and cultivated white dhamma. And if such people of black birth reached nibbana on account of their virtuous acts, colour became irrelevant, for they had then arrived at the nirvanic state of enlightenment which was neither black nor white. The person born white, i.e.

> born in a high-caste clan: noble, Brahman or householder, owning stately homes, riches, wealth, domains with gold and silver in plenty, means and service in plenty, corn and grain in plenty; and is well-formed, slightly pleasing, blessed with lily-like loveliness; is the recipient of food, drink, clothes, carriages, lovers, scents, ointments, bed, lodging, and lighting . . .

. . . could equally go the wrong way in the performance of his deeds, and so fall to hell at death for having accumulated black dhamma. Conversely, those of white birth would get to heaven if they practised white dhamma and reached the colour-free state of nibbana.[10] The Buddha's vanna, therefore, was a variation from black to colourless transparency based on both birth and deeds.

Such a view of life and its possibilities was a direct and obvious challenge to the Brahmanical framework. It was exacerbated by

---

[10] Ibid., pp. 274–5.

the Buddha's protest against the misery of poor people, especially the Chandalas who had been cast outside every hierarchy and were seen as beyond the pale. The *Matanga Jataka* tells the story of how a downtrodden Chandala named Matanga protested against oppression and taught a lesson to the Brahmanical establishment. The daughter of a merchant in the city of Benares – a conventional location in jataka stories – went to a park for some fun along with her maidservants. Even though Matanga stepped to one side of the road and stood quietly, as was expected of a Chandala, the merchant's daughter set her sights on him. Learning that she had happened to see a Chandala, the girl believed her eyes had been contaminated and therefore returned home to wash them. Her servants, disappointed at having lost their time of fun in the park, tortured Matanga until he lost consciousness. Awaking from his coma, Matanga went to her father's house and lay at his door. Replying to the question he was asked on why he lay there, Matanga said he wanted the daughter of the house. After seven days, afraid that his entire household would be contaminated, the family let the girl go. When the girl was ready to go with Matanga, he demanded that the girl carry him, for he had been badly hurt during the beating by her servants, so that she carried the Chandala, in full view of the people, to the Chandala settlement outside the city.[11] The moral of the story is of course to point the finger at the idiocy of the Brahmanical notion of purity whereby a merchant household feels compelled to give up a daughter because she has been contaminated by the mere presence of a Chandala. The story does not end there: the Chandala, now a saint, goes on to become an ascetic but manages to make his wife a wealthy woman with a son. Eventually, he has to be reborn in the form of ragged beggar in order to teach his son a lesson on the need to be kind to the poor. This Chandala saint is also suggested in the jataka as one of the Buddha's previous births. This indicates that even the lowly Chandalas were in the Buddhist worldview capable of eventually being reborn as the highest form of human beings

[11] *Jataka Stories*, no. 497, pp. 235–42.

The Chandalas who lived in city outskirts probably spoke a language barely intelligible to the city people they served. They likely came from communities outside the urban-rural settlements and had no opportunity to access high culture. Since the time of the Veda, Brahmans had thought of language-use as a signifier of clan status: the clans who accepted the authority of the Vedas were Indo-European speakers, even if they were never a unified political entity via military might.[12] By the time of the mid-first millennium BCE, communities of different cultures and languages appear in the service of city dwellers. The urban elites, much as today, did not communicate with them on spiritual matters or on things unrelated to their work. The Buddha's willingness to address every community regardless of its wealth or language is verbal iconoclasm directed against Brahman orthodoxy. He himself probably spoke Magadhi, the eastern Prakrit prevalent in the area where he preached, and the base for Pali, the canonical Buddhist language. But he is more concerned with the content of his message than the language used when instructing his monks to propagate his teaching. He claims that he himself engages his audiences in conversation by changing his own colour and language to suit that of his audience.[13] When advising his disciples on how to listen to his teachings, his constant emphasis is on the importance of the content: it does not matter if the language is not pleasing to the ear.[14] When instructing monks on how to speak he says:

> Monks: knowing a secret speech (*raho vāda*) that is not [either based in] fact, [or is] untrue, [or] not connected with the goal – one should not, if possible, utter that secret speech; and if, knowing that secret speech is fact, true, but not connected with the goal, he should train himself not to speak it. But if one knows that secret speech is fact, true, and connected with the goal, then he will know the right time to speak that secret speech . . .[15]

[12] Parasher, *Mlecchas in Early India*, p. 78.
[13] Ibid., p. 88; *Anguttara Nikāya*, VIII.Viii. 69, vol. IV, p. 205.
[14] *Majjhima Nikaya*, II, 240, vol. III, pp. 26–7.
[15] Ibid., III, 234, vol. III, p. 281.

Apart from being an implicit critique of the esotericism of Sanskrit, "the language of the gods", the secret language referred to, raho vada, could have been a language unknown to Buddhist preachers. Yakshas/Yakkhas were a category of people who did not speak the Indo-European languages – not even the Prakrit languages outside elite Brahman culture. This may also be connected to the fact that those who are often seen expressing their devotion on early Buddhist artworks show affiliations outside mainstream society. In the Bharhut Stupa railing pillars, it is apparent that those who joined the sangha were from the cult of the Yakkhas, such as the bandit we met earlier, Suchiloma. The chief of the Yakkhas, Kubera, who appears alongside the devas in the heaven of Thirty-three, appears also on the pillar showing veneration to the dome of the stupa.

Worshippers of the Naga cult were among the groups who spoke languages other than the Indo-European. These Naga communities were widespread in the Greater Magadha region, the frontier of Vedic culture. The Sanchi Stupa built by Ashoka as an outreach for the extension of Buddhism into the Naga and other cults, as well as the forest people (Atavi), was probably just a barren dome. The artworks on the railings and four gates surrounding the dome are mostly a consequence of donations by local people, including the Yakkhas and Nagas who continued to follow the sangha after Ashoka, and even after the end of the Mauryan regime. On the middle beam of the southern gate a royal figure with his retinue proceeds to the stupa in the centre to pay homage; from the opposite direction a king with a hood of cobras bows to touch the stupa. The royal figure is almost certainly Ashoka, who is also depicted on smaller panels made by ivory workers from Vedisa, a town new in Mauryan times. Ivory carvers lived off forest resources, and Vedisa became the capital of the Sunga Dynasty, which was averse to Buddhism and succeeded the Mauryans. The Naga affiliation with Buddhism seems to have continued all the same, and much later we have both Nagarjuna, the earliest theologian of Mahayana Buddhism, and Nagasena, the pandit who debated with the Greek king Menander. Some Nagas, we have also noted, are seen positioned within the Pali texts and on the panel of the Bharhut Stupa in the heaven of Thirty-three Devas (Fig. 14).

The Realm of Asuras

After the two groups of Indo-European speakers diverged around the mid-second millennium BCE, systematic deviations in their language developed, as in the case of ahura and asura. The Iranian "h" corresponds to the Indian "s": for example, the "h" in the Iranian *daha* is the "s" in the Indian *dasa*. There is even an argument from the side of the Indians which suggests that because asuras mispronounced words, they lost their battle with the devas.[16]

By the time cities had sprouted on the North Indian plains, the two branches of the Indo-European languages were no longer mutually comprehensible. However, the ahuras never stopped percolating into India: many came in when the Achaemenid Persians established their two subcontinental satraps, Hindush and Gandara. Taxila, as noted, became the interface of Zoroastrian and Vedic traditions and flourished as a cultural centre. The Zoroastrians of the Persian Empire who filtered into India were soldiers, priests, traders, and artisans. Their presence on Buddhist monuments means they were a definite presence in the region of the

Fig. 15: Sanchi – Ashoka and Naga king worship the Buddha, American Institute of Indian Studies, no. A3.12.

[16] Parasher, *Mlecchas in Early India*, p. 84.

Buddhist communities. A Persian-looking statue, made by a certain Mahila, on one of the rail pillars around Bharhut stands in the same way as do those of Yakkhas and Devakas, i.e. both as worshippers of the Buddha and as representatives of their own community (see Fig. 5). Buddhists, it seems, also found place for these asuras within their idea of the universe: they positioned them at a level lower than humans but higher than animals.

The Realm of Animals

The Buddhist sangha often gathered to meditate in the outskirts of cities and villages and shared these public spaces with other sects. In effect this meant being close to nature, and familiarity with nature and the animal world. So we find that, within the concept of Buddhist rebirth, to be an animal is not necessarily the worst fate, but only an episode in the larger cycle of lives and rebirths. The Buddha himself, the jataka stories tell us, had been born in the form of various animals, such as the self-sacrificing six-tusked white elephant, and the wise and courageous monkey king Mahakapi. The Naga cult which worshipped the cobra provides another example: snakes were ubiquitous, their presence both feared and respected. The Buddha had notions on the different forms of Nagas: "The egg-born, the womb-born (*jalabuja*), the sweat-born (*sanseda-ja*), those born without parents (*opapatika*)."[17] The egg-born was the cobra; the womb-born was the Naga in human shape; the sweat-born seems to refer to a myth; and those without parents probably refers to the supernatural form of the Naga, and to its earthly shape as the Naga cult. The Buddha also elaborated on the transitions between the egg-born and the womb-born. If the egg-born Nagas observed Uposatha – the day preceding the four stages of the moon's waxing and waning, when monks and nuns congregated – they would rid themselves of bad habits and be transformed into the womb-born. And if womb-born Nagas fell into

---

[17] *Sanyutta Nikaya*, XXIX, 1, p. 192.

bad habits and treaded the primrose path of dalliance, they would slip backwards into the Naga's egg-born form.[18]

The story of Erapata the Nagaraja illustrates this process of transitions. This Erapata reverted to the cobra form on account of sins in his former lives. In order to resume his human form, he needed to listen to the teachings of the Buddha. However, he did not know the whereabouts of the Buddha. So he held his beautiful daughter out of the stretch of water where he was situated in order to attract passing travellers who might help him search for the Buddha: this tale is depicted on a Bharhut panel (Fig. 17). A Bodhi tree on the left-bottom side represents the Buddha, the Nagaraja being the man wearing a five-headed cobra crown and kneeling in front of the Bodhi tree. Three figures stand behind the Nagaraja: a man who wears a hood with four cobra heads, a woman who wears two cobra heads, and a woman who wears a single cobra head. This was the Naga clan's way of displaying its hierarchy – by the numbers of cobra heads on a hood.

Of the many Nagarajas in Buddhist literature, some became legendary: Nagaraja Mucilinda, the Naga who protected Sakyamuni's meditation in Uruvela village, is also presented under the Bodhi tree (Fig. 18). These legends persisted among Buddhists for a very long time, including among the Mahayana branch. When Buddhism reached China and the Chinese found it difficult to revere cobra snakes as gods, they altered the Nagas into dragons.[19]

The Realm of Ghosts and Hell

Only the most incorrigibly sinful are condemned to live in hell. *Niraya*, *nir-aya*, or hell, is the opposite of *nir-vana*, the eternal liberation from suffering. There are several hells in Pali literature, with avici niraya the most fearful, the most fortified, and the hardest to escape. The small mercy is that even condemnation to this level of

---

[18] Ibid., 3, p. 193.
[19] Liu, "Naga and Dragon", pp. 183–97.

Fig. 16: Bharhut – "Aya Isidinasa Bhanakasa (reciter) danam. Erapato nagaraja Bhagavato Vadate", Indian Museum, no. 265, American Institute of Indian Studies, no. 483.99.

hell, as to other hells, is not eternal. In the Buddha's own lifetime, his worst adversary, as we have seen, was Devadatta, who tried to assassinate the Buddha and take over leadership of the sangha. Failing in this, he attempted dissension and a separate sangha. The treachery notwithstanding, the Buddha tried to change his enemy's mind with the argument that dividing the sangha would condemn him to the hell for a kalpa – a massive period of cosmic time (*kappatthikam*). Conversely, if he made peace, he would be reborn in

Fig. 17: Sanchi – Nagaraja Mucilinda, American Institute of Indian Studies, no. 320.90.

heaven.[20] Devadatta seems not to have been persuaded of either likelihood and led 500 monks astray to set up a new sangha. After his sudden death, Sariputta and Moggallana led the 500 monks back to the Buddha's Bamboo Garden, where the sage gave his brothers a dressing down before admitting them back into the sangha. He told them then that Devadatta had fallen into the well-fortified avici version of hell.[21] When another monk, Kokaliya, tried to cause a schism in the sangha by slandering the elders Sariputta

[20] *Vinaya Texts,* part III, Cullavagga, VII, 3, 16, p. 254.
[21] Ibid., 4.8, p. 264.

and Moggallana, the Buddha gave a vivid description of torture in the many hells that existed. In all these versions of hell, however, the duration for which the person is condemned is obscurely long but never an eternity.[22] By and large, this imagery of hells seems to have been deployed to discipline monks and very rarely used in teachings to audiences outside the sangha.

Falling below the realm of animals but not quite in hell were petas and petis, homeless spirits. Peta derived from *pitr*, the Sanskrit word for forefather, which evolved into *preta*, which even now denotes a ghost in Hindi. Both peta and preta mean a departed spirit who wanders morosely, unable to find stable dwelling after leaving this world. A late Pali canonical text, *Peta-Vatthu: Stories of the Departed*, is devoted to the problems of homeless spirits. The etymology of peta shows the connection between such lost spirits and ancestors. In the Buddhist rebirth scheme, a peta or peti could well be the father or mother of someone still alive, or an ancestor in one of his or her previous lives. In ancestor-worshipping societies, ritual sacrifices could appease these restless ancestral souls. But the Buddhist sangha's opposition to this idea of ritual appeasement is evident even from the fact that it gathered together individuals who had left their homes in the present world: the effort was a kind of practice not only against the ancestor-worshipping tradition but also at impeding any emotional expression of filial piety. Monks who joined the sangha had thus to face the dilemma of pursuing either the spiritual goal of nirvana or the obligation of taking care of their elderly.

To address this conflict, the *Peta-Vatthu* includes a story about the futile effort to feed an ancestor who has already departed. A householder is overcome by grief when his father passes away. His son Sujata designs a way of consoling his father. He tries to feed a dead ox grass and water; this is odd behaviour and it attracts the attention of passers-by. When the ghost of the householder hears of this, he believes his son has gone mad and rushes to the location of

---

[22] *Sutta Nipata*, 10, *Kokaliyasutta*, pp. 116–22.

the dead ox. Here his wise son Sujata explains to his confused father that weeping over the departed is as futile as feeding a dead ox.[23]

In place of futile ritual, the Buddha, according to the *Peta-Vatthu*, prescribes donations to the sangha as the best way to help petas and petis because the merit of giving can be transferred to the dear departed.[24] A peti who had in an earlier birth been the mother of Sariputta the Elder fell into a peti status because she had abused a travelling monk at a time when her husband was away. Sariputta then managed to transfer merit to her out of Bimbisara's charity to the sangha.[25] Stories of this variety, loaded with clear messages and concocted at some point after the Buddha, encouraged donations to the sangha as the most effective replacement for rituals in people's efforts to help the spirits of deceased kinfolk.

When the Buddhist sangha expanded to regions in South Asia and eventually to all corners of Asia, hierarchical structures came into being within various institutions in many of the regions. But there was never a pan-Buddhist hierarchy – neither in theory nor in practice. And the status of monks and nuns in monastic hierarchies was never allowed to be based on birth: it was more or less based on spiritual attainment and scholastic achievement in the field of Buddhist knowledge.

Fig 18: Sujata feeds a dead ox, Bharhut, Indian Museum, 325–7, American Institute of Indian Studies, neg. no. 483.1.

[23] *Peta-Vatthu*, I, 8, pp. 14–16.
[24] Ibid., 4-5, pp. 6–11.
[25] *Peta-Vatthu*, II, 2, pp. 29–32.

10

Sanchi and Bharhut

Visual Memories of Early Buddhist Society

Some hundred years or more after the passing of the Buddha, the Magadha-based family of the Mauryas (Mauryan Dynasty) unified the polities scattered between the Ganges and Indus valleys, and extended their rule southwards into a large portion of peninsular India to form the first empire of South Asia. The Mauryan Empire established a patriarchal dynastic order but the principle of primogeniture was probably not strictly followed. The third king of the Mauryans, Ashoka (r. circa 268–232 BCE) ruled a vast country with numerous ethnic communities speaking a variety of languages and worshipping many different deities. After conquering Kalinga (in contemporary Odisha), the last piece of territory acquired by the Mauryans, Ashoka issued his famous edicts stating his conception of the empire and his policy of compassionate rule. He addressed his subjects as "Brahmanas and Shramanas, those of other sects, householders, and Greeks". Expressing remorse for the Kalinga war, he warned the forest people, the Atavi, that he would suppress them if they made trouble for his regime.[1] He also made clear that he was a follower of the Buddha and intended to implement the Buddhist egalitarian ideas of peace and harmony.

---

[1] The translation is an incorporation of various versions spread across India: see Appendix V in Thapar, *Asoka and the Decline of the Mauryans*, pp. 255–7. The original edicts are in Hultzsch, *Inscriptions of Asoka*, p. 9.

Facing the disputes of various religious sects vying for his patronage, he also issued an edict specifically to address this issue:

> The Beloved of the Gods, the king Piyadassi, honours all sects and both ascetics and laymen, with gifts and various forms of recognition. But the Beloved of the Gods does not consider gifts or honour to be as important as the advancement of the essential doctrine of all sects. This progress of the essential doctrine takes many forms, but its basis is the control of one's speech, so as not to extol one's own sect or disparage another's on unsuitable occasions, or at least to do so only mildly on certain occasions. On each occasion one should honour another man's sect, for by doing so one increases the influence of one's own sect and benefits that of the other man; while by doing otherwise one diminishes the influence of one's own sect and harms the other man's . . .[2]

In keeping with this, Ashoka's largesse was not restricted to the Buddhist sangha but spread across various sects. The rock caves around Gaya and Rajgir reveal that Ashoka and his grandson Dasaratha donated several of these well-excavated caves to Ajivaka ascetics.[3] Ashoka's world achievements, however, disappeared from the memory of Indians after the demise of the Mauryan Empire and the exit of Buddhism from South Asia. Nevertheless, forest people and those living on the peripheries of the empire remembered him – and therefore also the Buddha – long after his passing, thanks to the existence of the Buddhist sangha's mediations between the metropolitan world and the territories beyond.

Among the stupas verified as built by Ashoka is the Sanchi Stupa, located at the border area of the Magadha region and wooded mountains. The railings surrounding the stupa are covered in artistic relief work with Buddhist themes and motifs that depict various creatures – elephants, lions, peacocks, Yakshis. Beams and pillars on the four gates, and on railings surrounding the stupa dome, display scenes from stories of early Buddhist society. Naga kings

---

[2] Appendix V, 12th Major Rock Edict, in Thapar, *Asoka and the Decline of the Mauryas*, p. 255.
[3] Falk, *Asokan Sites and Artefacts*, pp. 255–82.

crowned with a cobra showing multiple heads appear on many panels; donors with the names of Naga cults confirm that Naga worshippers became followers of the Buddha. There are names associated with the Yakkha cult of nearby areas; and Greek names, indicating the origin of donors in places as far off as Gandhara and Kamboja. The obvious inference is that the Sanchi stupas, and the monasteries developed there, had been a hub of communication for the world of Buddhism.[4] Certainly, the popularity of the location is suggested by the fact that after all the space in the first stupa had been filled with artwork, two more stupas and a monastery were added to the complex, which shows evidence of activity all the way down to the Kushan period in the early years CE.

Buddhist followers in the environs of Vedisa, a town bordering agricultural area and forests, were among the major donors of these

Fig. 19: Stupa 1 – Sanchi, general view from the south-east, American Institute of Indian Studies, neg. no. A36.68, courtesy of the Library of the University of Pennsylvania.

[4] Marshall, *et al.*, Chapter XXI: Votive Inscriptions, *The Monuments of Sanchi*, vol. I, pp. 297–9.

artworks which offer respect to the memory of Ashoka as Chakarvartin – the sacred king who turns the wheel of the Buddha's dhamma. On the east face of the left pillar of the southern gate, ivory workers from Vedisa carved two panels showing Ashoka paying respect to the Buddha's relics (Fig. 20).

Vedisakehi daṁtakarehi
Rupa kaṁmaṁ kataṁ

Fig. 20: Sanchi Stupa 1, Southern Gate, east face of left pillar, showing Ashoka's visit to Bodh Gaya and worship of the hair and turban of the Buddha, American Institute of Indian Studies, neg. A3.33, courtesy of the Library of the University of Pennsylvania.

Meanwhile, scenes on several relief panels record political events that are believed to have taken place during the time of the Buddha. There is the procession of Bimbisara, the first royal patron of the Buddha, going out of his capital city Rajagaha in his chariot to pay homage to the Buddha (Fig. 21).

Pasenadi, the king of Kosala who sought the Buddha's advice from time to time, also appears (Fig. 22).

Fig. 21: Bimbisara, king of Magadha, going out of the city of Rajagaha, Sanchi Stupa 1, northern gate, east pillar of west face, American Institute of Indian Studies, neg. 320.56, courtesy of the Library of the University of Pennsylvania.

Fig. 22: Royal procession of Pasenadi going out of the city of Savatthi, Sanchi Stupa 1, northern gate, north side of the east pillar, American Institute of Indian Studies, neg. no. 239.19, courtesy of the Library of the University

A battle among the rajas over the Buddha's relics is another commemorative piece. The back view of the bottom beam of the southern gate displays an elaborate and large-scale battle – this scene could of course be a more general representation of the warfare of the time (Fig. 23).

The Bharhut Stupa, which flourished on the route linking Vedisa to the Ganges, is not connected with Ashoka's patronage; the

Fig. 23: Battle for the relics of the Buddha, Sanchi Stupa 1, southern gate, north face of lower beam, American Institute of Indian Studies, neg. no. 321.14, courtesy of the Library of the University of Pennsylvania.

Sungas, who ruled when the artworks around it were set up, were in fact Brahmans. But they do not seem to have thwarted Buddhists from practising their beliefs, and the railings surrounding the Bharhut Stupa are even more majestic than those in Sanchi (Fig. 24).

A queen named Nagarakhita made a donation here.[5] A royal figure holding a reliquary on his horse is carved on the first pillar, donated by a woman from Vedisa.[6] The artistic style of the Bharhut Stupa is slightly different from the stupas at Sanchi, but the theme of the art is similar in its homage to the heroes of Buddhism. The major structural difference between the two is that the pillars at Bharhut are wide and high enough to provide space for human-sized figures. Sirima Devata, who rose from being courtesan of Rajagaha to the heaven of the devas, stands in a pillar worshipping the stupa, and is in turn worshipped by women hoping to be elevated to heaven (see Fig. 6). Devata Culacoka, a deity from the wild, stands on an elephant holding a tree (Fig. 25), the pillar a gift made by "Aya (Arya) Panthkasa".[7] This and several other devatas, not found in

[5] *Bharhut Inscriptions*, A.4(882), pp. 1–2; Plate II, p. 15.
[6] American Institute of Indian Studies, no. 249.92, courtesy of the Library of the University of Pennsylvania.
[7] *Bharhut Inscriptions*, B11, A71, XVI Plates, x, xxxii, pp. 42–3; Indian Museum, Calcutta, no. 62, American Institute of Indian Studies, neg. 484.28, courtesy of the Library of the University of Pennsylvania.

Fig. 24: Bharhut Stupa, great railing, Indian Museum, Calcutta, nos 107–41, American Institute of Indian Studies, neg. no. A36.85, courtesy of the Library of the University of Pennsylvania.

the Pali texts, were very likely related to cults that were introduced to Buddhism by local communities.

One of the women shown in the tree-holding posture is called Yakkhi; another is is Cada Yakkhi, who stands on a sheep and holds a tree (Fig. 26).[8] Cada Yakkhi shares her pillar with Khupira Yakkha.

Several famous Yakkhas became gods on the pillars of the Bharhut Stupa: Khupira, Suchiloma, and Virudhaka – the last being Lord of the Kumbandas who ruled the South as one of the four guardians of the heaven (Fig. 27).[9]

In addition to these Yakkhas, who are well recorded in the Pali

---

[8] *Bharhut Inscriptions*, B2, Plates, xxix, xxx, xvi, p. 74, Calcutta Indian Museum, no. 106, American Institute of Indian Studies, neg. no. 243.38, courtesy of the Library of the University of Pennsylvania.

[9] *Dīgha Nikāya*, II.207, p. 242; photo, Indian Museum, Calcutta, no. 197, American Institute of Indian Studies, neg. 483.94, courtesy of the Library of the University of Pennsylvania.

Fig. 25: Devata Culacoka, great railing Bharhut Stupa,
Indian Museum, Calcutta no. 62, American Institute of Indian Studies,
neg. 484.28, courtesy of the Library of the University
of Pennsylvania.

texts, there are some like Gangito Yakkho who have not been identified in that corpus. His name suggests a local deity related to the river Ganges (Fig. 28). In this sense, the artworks of early Buddhism are a vital source of information which supplement the textual and literary sources.

Among the Nagarajas depicted on the Bharhut Stupa, the name Cakavako Nagaraja has not been located in the Pali texts. The

Fig. 26: Cada Yakkhi, Bharhut Stupa, great railing, Indian Museum, Calcutta, no. 106, American Institute of Indian Studies, neg. no. 243.38, courtesy of the Library of the University of Pennsylvania.

statue here shows a man with a five-cobras headgear, and an item that looks like an empty quiver wrapped with feathers is tied to his left arm, suggesting a majestic king of the forest (Fig. 29). The Magadhi name Cakavako could well be Cakravatin, the title for the ideal Buddhist ruler.

The Bharhut Stupa is also famous for its numerous relief panels depicting jataka stories. Many of them were well remembered, such

Fig. 27: Virudhaka Yakkho, Bharhut great railing pillar, Indian Museum, Calcutta, no. 197, American Institute of Indian Studies, neg. 483.94, courtesy of the Library of the University of Pennsylvania.

as the Mahakapi Jataka (no. 401), in which the king of the monkeys uses his body to form a bridge between trees across a river to allow his clan to escape danger. The last monkey, who is evil, strikes him down after crossing. The gods prevent the tragedy by holding

Fig. 28: Gangito Yakkho, great railing pillar, Calcutta, Indian Museum, no. 199, American Institute of Indian Studies, neg. no. 483.88, courtesy of the Library of the University of Pennsylvania.

a canvas to stop the fall of Mahakapi (Fig. 30).[10] This panel, like most story panels in Buddhist art, shrinks many story lines into a single image, which means a story-telling guide was probably needed to explain the depiction to visiting audiences. The correlation

[10] Indian Museum, Calcutta, no. 35, American Institute of Indian Studies, neg. no. 482.83.

Fig. 29: Cakavako Nagaraja,, Indian Museum, Calcutta, no. 195, American Institute of Indian Studies, neg. 244.66, courtesy of the Library of the University of Pennsylvania.

between jataka tales on these stupas and the Pali jataka literature show that story-telling and artistic illustration were parallel processes after Mauryan times – at least in the peripheral regions where culturally different communities met.

Despite decades of scholarly research on the Bharhut Stupa, many of the stories on the panels remain undeciphered. Two panels on crossbars of the great railings show a group of monkeys

Fig. 30: Mahakapi Jataka, great railing, pillar, Calcutta, Indian Museum, no. 35, American Institute of Indian Studies, neg. no. 482.83.

capturing an elephant: one depicts the capturing, the other a triumphal march with the captured elephant (Fig. 31).[11] The man who donated the medallion on the bottom had his gift recorded:

Vidisāta bhutarakhitasa dānam

This is the gift of Bhutakhita from Vedisa.[12]

---

[11] Bharhut Stupa, great railing, south-west crossbar, medallion, Indian Museum, Calcutta, 164, American Institute of Indian Studies, neg. no. 244.15; Indian Museum, Calcutta, no. 119, American Institute of Indian Studies, neg. no. 482.97.

[12] *Bharhut Inscriptions*, A31, Plate V, p. 25.

31a

31b

Fig. 31a and Fig. 31b. Monkeys capturing elephant, Bharhut Stupa, great railing crossbar, Indian Museum, Calcutta, 164, American Institute of Indian Studies, neg. no. 244.15; Indian Museum, no. 119, American Institute of Indian Studies neg. no. 482.97.

The donor's name indicates he was protected by a bhuta, so that his origins were within a Bhuta cult. When he made this donation, he was a resident of Vedisa, where he had become a Buddhist. Could this story of monkeys and a captured elephant have followed him from the Bhuta culture into the river of Buddhist tales?

A Persian-looking statue on a pillar was donated by a "bhadatamahila" (Goodman Mahirakkhita?: see Fig. 5).[13] This asura patron stands apart from all the other human-sized figures on the major pillars and could be an outsider, a merchant perhaps, who joined the local Buddhist community and apparently spent a large sum to have himself repositioned with a high status in the local community.

In sum, visual memories in the shape of the artworks of the Sanchi and Bharhut stupas, alongside early Buddhist monuments in general, contain stories and information that circulated among Buddhist communities for more than 2000 years. Some of the early Buddhist literature may have been the source of artistic inspiration for the artists and patrons of these artworks. Some probably derive from memories handed down from the time of the Buddha; others were probably collected by those who joined the sangha, or by lay communities with their own memories of the past.

Taken as a whole, early Buddhist art and literature give us glimpses into the lived life of early Indian societies in the time of the Buddha, and of Buddhist devotees in his aftermath.

---

[13] *Bharhut Inscriptions Corpus*, A65, Plates XXXI, IX, pp. 40–1, courtesy of the Library of the University of Pennsylvania.

Bibliography

Pali Canon Referred to in the Text

Anguttara-Nikāya, I.14, §26, in *The Book of the Gradual Sayings*, vol. I, trans. F.L. Woodward (The Pali Text Society, London: Routledge & Kegan Paul, 1979).

Bṛhadāraṇyaka Upaniṣad, in *Upaniṣads*, trans. Patrick Olivelle (New York: Oxford University Press, 1996).

The Dhammapada, trans. and ed. Valerie Roebuck (Harmondsworth: Penguin Classics, 2010).

Dīgha Nikāya: Dialogues of the Buddha, from the Pali text, trans. T.W. Rhys Davids (London: The Pali Text Society, 1899; rpntd London: Routledge & Kegan Paul, 1977).

Jataka Stories, ed. E.B. Cowell, trans. from the Pali by Robert Chalmers, *et al.* (Cambridge: Cambridge University Press, 1895; rpntd Pali Text Society, London: Routledge & Kegan Paul, 1973).

Majjhima-Nikaya: The Collection of the Middle Length Sayings, vol. III, translated from the Pali by I.B. Horner (The Pali Text Society, London: Routledge & Kegan Paul, 1977).

Peta-Vatthu: Stories of the Departed, translated from the Pali by Henry Snyder Gehman, in *Minor Anthologies of the Pali Canon* (London: Pali Text Society, 1942; rpntd London: Routledge and Kegan Paul, 1974).

Sabbāsava Sutta [All the Asavas], translated by T.W. Rhys Davids, in *Buddhist Sutras* (Oxford: Oxford University Press, 1881; rpntd Delhi: Motilal Banarsidass, 1980).

Sanyutta-Nikaya: The Book of the Kindred Sayings, translated by F.L. Woodward (The Pali Text Society, London: Routledge & Kegan Paul, 1979).

The Sutta-Nipāta: A Collection of Discourses, translated from the Pali by V. Fausboll, in *Sacred Books of the East*, vol. 10 (Oxford: Oxford University Press, 1881; rpntd Delhi: Motilal Banarsidass, 1980).

Therīgāthā, Psalms of the Early Buddhists, I; Psalms of the Sisters, Theragāthā, II; Psalms of the Brethren, trans. Mrs Rhys Davids (London: The Pali Text Society, 1909; rpntd London: Routledge & Kegan Paul, 1980).
Udana, in *The Minor Anthologies of the Pali Canon,* II, trans. F.L. Woodward (London: Pali Text Society, 1935; rpntd 1985).
Vimanavatthu: The Minor Anthologies of the Pali Canon, IV translated from the Pali by I.B. Horner (Pali Text Society, London: Routledge & Kegan Paul, 1974).
Vinaya Texts, translated from the Pali by T.W. Rhys Davids (Oxford: Oxford University Press, 1885; rpntd Delhi: Motilal Banarsidass, 1975).

Inscriptional Sources

Bharhut Inscriptions, in *Corpus Inscriptionum Indicarum,* vol. II, pt II, ed. H. Lüders, revised E. Waldschmidt and M.A. Mehendale (Archaeological Survey of India, 1963).
Inscriptions of Asoka, ed. and transl. E. Hultzsch, vol. I of *Corpus Inscriptionum Indicarum* (Indian Government Publications, new edn Delhi: Indological Book House, 1969).
Marshall, John, and Alfred Foucher, *The Monuments of Sanchi,* inscriptions by N.G. Majumdar (Delhi: Swati Publications, 1982).

Visual Sources of Ancient Indian Monuments

Photo Archives of the American Institute of Indian Studies, in the Library of the University of Pennsylvania.

Secondary Sources

Abdullaev, Kazim, "Sacred Plants and the Cultic Beverage Haoma", *Comparative Studies of South Asia, Africa and the Middle East,* vol. 30, no. 3, 2010.
Arrian, *The Campaigns of Alexander,* trans. Aubrey de Selincourt 1958, revised J.R. Hamilton (Harmondsworth: Penguin Books, 1971).
Agrawala, V.S., *India as Known to Pāṇini: A Study of the Cultural Material in the Ashṭādhyāyī* (Lucknow: University of Lucknow, 1953).
Ashṭādhyāyī of Pāṇini, trans. and ed. Srisa Chandra Vasu (Delhi: Motilal Banarsidass, 1891; rpntd 1988).

Boyce, Mary, *Zoroastrians: Their Religious Beliefs and Practices* (London and New York: Routledge, 2001).
Brancaccio, Pia, "Aṅgulimāla or the Taming of the Forest", *East and West*, vol. 49, no. 1/4 (December 1999).
Bronkhorst, Johannes, *Greater Magadha: Studies in the Culture of Early India* (Leiden: Brill, 2007).
Cardona, George, "Panini's Dates and the Evidence of Coinage", *Indological Research Different Standpoints*, ed. P.C. Muraleemadhavan (Delhi: New Bharatiya Book Corporation, 2013).
Chakravarti, Uma, *On the Social Philosophy of Buddhism* (Shimla: Indian Institute of Advanced Study, 2015).
Coogan, Michael D., ed., *The New Oxford Annotated Bible*, 3rd edn (New York: Oxford University Press, 2002).
Curtis, John E., and Nigel Tallis, *Forgotten Empire: The World of Ancient Persia* (Berkeley: University of California Press, 2005).
Decaroli, Robert, *Haunting the Buddha: Indian Popular Religions and the Formation of Buddhism* (Oxford: Oxford University Press, 2004).
Falk, Harry, *Asokan Sites and Artefacts* (Mainz am Rhem: Verlag Philipp von Zabern, 2006).
Falk, Harry, "Soma I and II", *Bulletin of the School of Oriental and African Studies*, vol. 52, University of London (1989).
Fargard VI, The Zend-Avesta, trans. James Darmesteter (Oxford: Oxford University Press, 1887; rpntd Delhi: Motilal Banarsidass, 1980).
Gautama, *Institutes of the Sacred Law*, in *the Sacred Laws of the Aryas*, pt I, trans. George Bühler (Oxford: Clarendon Press, 1879; rpntd Delhi: Motilal Banarsidass, 1975).
Ghosh, A., *The City in Early Historical India* (Calcutta: Indian Institute of Advanced Study, 1973).
Glass, Andrew, "A Preliminary Study of Kharoshthi Manuscript Paleography", Master's Thesis, University of Washington, Department of Asian Languages and Literature, 2000.
Grihya Sutras, Rules of Vedic Domestic Ceremonies, II, 8.1–10, trans. Hermann Oldenberg (Oxford: Oxford University Press, 1886; rpntd Delhi: Motilal Banarsidass, 1981).
Hallock, Richard T., *The Persepolis Fortification Tablets* (Chicago: University of Chicago Press, 1969).
Hawkes, Jason, and Akira Shimada, eds, *Buddhist Stupas in South Asia* (New Delhi: Oxford University Press, 2009).

Henkelman, Wouter F.M., "Cyrus the Persian and Darius the Elamite: A Case of Mistaken Identity", in *Herodotus and the Persian Empire,* ed. Robert Rollinger, Brigitte Truschnegg, Reinhold Bichler (Wiesbaden: Harrassowitz Verlag, 2011).

Herodotus, *The Histories,* VII 65, trans. G.C. Macaulay, revised Donald Lateiner (New York: Barnes & Noble Classics, 2004).

Horner, I.B., *Women Under Primitive Buddhism* (Delhi: Oriental Publisher & Distributors, 1975).

Kahneman, Daniel, *Thinking, Fast and Slow* (New York: Farrar, Straus, and Giroux, 2011).

Kautiliya Arthasastra, ed. and trans. R.P. Kangle (Bombay: University of Bombay, 1965–72).

Konow, Sten, ed., *Kharoshthi Inscriptions* (Varanasi: Indological Book House, 1969).

Laws of Manu, trans. George Bühler (Oxford: Oxford University Press, 1886; rpntd Delhi: Motilal Banarsidass, 1979).

Liu, Xinru, "Naga and Dragon: An Animal Cult in Ancient India and Central Asia", in *Archivum Eurasiae Medii Aevi,* ed. P.B. Golden, R.K. Kovalev, A.P. Martinea, J. Skaff, and A. Zimonyi, 21 (2014–15), Wiesbaden: Harrassowitz Verlag.

Marshall, John, *Taxila* (Cambridge: Cambridge University Press 1951; rpntd Delhi: Motilal Banarsidass, 1975).

Marshall, John, & Alfred Foucher, inscriptions ed. and trans. N.G. Majumdar, *The Monuments of Sanchi* (Delhi: Swati Publications, rpntd 1982).

McCrindle, John W., *Ancient India as Described in Classical Literature* (New Delhi: Oriental Books Reprint Corporation, 1979).

Meng Ren, Zihua Tang, Xinhua Wu, *et al.*, "The Origins of Cannabis Smoking: Chemical Residue Evidence from the First Millennium BCE in the Pamirs", *Science Advances,* 5, 12 (June 2019).

Parasher, Aloka, *Mlecchas in Early India: A Study in Attitudes Towards Outsiders upto AD 600* (New Delhi: Munshiram Manoharial Publishers, 1991).

Ray, Himanshu Prabha, "The Archaeology of Stupas: Constructing Buddhist Identity in the Colonial Period", in *Buddhist Stupas in South Asia,* ed. Jason Hawkes & Akira Shimada (New Delhi: Oxford University Press, 2009).

Salomon, Richard, *Ancient Buddhist Scrolls from Gandhara, the British*

Library Kharoshti Fragments (Seattle: University of Washington Press, 1999).
Satapatha Brahmana, trans. Julius Eggeling, pt v (Oxford: Clarendon Press, 1900; rpntd Delhi: Motilal Banarsidass, 1978).
Shaked, Shaul, *Le satrape de Bactriane et son gouverneur, Documents araméens du IVe S. avant notre ère provenant de Bactriane* (Paris: De Boccard, 2004).
Sharma, J.P., *Republics in Ancient India* (Leiden: Brill, 1968).
Schwartzberg, Joseph, *A Historical Atlas of South Asia* (Chicago: University of Chicago Press 1978).
Sekhera, Kalalelle, *Early Buddhist Sanghas and Viharas in Sri Lanka (up to 4th Century A.D.)* (Varanasi: Rishi Publications, 1998).
Sharma, J.P., *Republics in Ancient India* (Leiden: E.J. Brill, 1968).
Skilling, Peter, "Scriptural Authenticity and the Śrāvaka Schools: An Essay Towards an Indian Perspective", *The Eastern Buddhist*, 2010, new series, vol. 41, no. 2 (2010), 1–47, Eastern Buddhist Society, Stable URL: https://www.jstor.org/stable/44362554.
Staal, Frits, "How a Psychoactive Substance Becomes a Ritual: The Case of Soma", *Social Research*, vol. 68, no. 3 (Fall 2001).
Strabo XV.1.61, in John W. McCrindle, *Ancient India as Described in Classical Literature* (New Delhi: Oriental Books Reprint Corporation, 1979).
Thapar, Romila, *Asoka and the Decline of the Mauryas* (Delhi: Oxford University Press, 1961).
Thapar, Romila *From Lineage to State* (Delhi: Oxford University Press, 1984).
Thapar, Romila, *Cultural Pasts: Essays in Early Indian History* (New Delhi: Oxford University Press, 2000).
Thapar, Romila, *Sakuntala: Texts, Readings, Histories* (London: Anthem Press, 2002).
Thapar, Romila, *The Past Before Us: Historical Traditions of Early North India* (Ranikhet: Permanent Black, 2013).
Upaniṣads, trans. Patrick Olivelle (New York: Oxford University Press, 1996).
Vasistha Dharmasastra, trans. George Bühler, in the *Sacred Laws of the Aryas*, trans. George Bühler (Oxford: Clarendon Press, 1879; rpntd Delhi: Motilal Banarsidass, 1975).
Vasu, Srisa Chandra, trans. and ed., *The Aṣṭādhyāyī of Pāṇini* (Delhi: Motilal Banarsidass, rpntd 1988).

"Vendīdād", Fargard I, 13 (45), *The Zend-Avesta*, trans. James Darmesteter (Oxford: Oxford University Press, 1887; rpntd Delhi: Motilal Banarsidass, 1980).

Walters, Jonathan, "Communal Karma and Karmic Community in Theravada Buddhist History", in *Constituting Communities: Theravada Buddhism and the Religious Cultures of South and Southeast Asia*, ed. John Clifford Holt, Jacob N. Kinnard, and Jonathan S. Wasters (Albany: State University of New York Press, 2003).

Wang, Binghua, Gumugou [Valley of Ancient Graves], (Urumuchi: Xinjiang Renmin Chubanshe, 2014). 王炳华《古墓沟》乌鲁木齐：新疆人民出版社，2014 年

Whitehouse, H., P. François, P.E Savage, *et al.*, "Complex Societies Precede Moralizing Gods Throughout World History", *Nature*, 568 (2019).

Wu Xinhua, and Tang Zihua, "Jirzankal Cemetery Covered with Rows of Black-and-White Stones: Key Excavations and Primary Research", *Eurasian Studies*, English Edition, IV, ed. Yu Taishan and Li Jinxiu, Center for Eurasian Studies, Chinese Academy of Social Sciences (Beijing, 2016).

Xuanzang and Bianji, *Da Tang Xiyu Ji Jiaozhu* [Xuanzang's Tang Dynasty Account of [his] Journey to the West, edited and annotated], 玄奘、辩机原著，季羡林等校注《大唐西域记校注》ed. Ji Xianlin, *et al.* (Beijing: Zhonghua Shuju, 1985).

Yijing, *Nanhai Jiguinei Fa Zhuan Jiaozhu* [Buddhist Dharma Brought Back from the South Sea], ed. Wang Bangwei (Beijing: Zhonghua Shuju, 1995).

Index

acchara/s 20, 88, 161; *see also* apsara
Achaemenid Persia 28, 30, 32, 34, 36, 38, 44, 47, 48, 50, 51, 66, 67, 173
Afghanistan 2, 9, 15, 34, 68, 69, 167
ahura/s 15, 26–49, 66, 173
Ai-Khanoum 9
Ajatasattu (Ajatashatru) 12, 94ff., 101ff., 114, 123, 129, 131, 132, 138
Alambusa 89, 161
Alexander of Macedonia 9, 34, 36, 36n
Ambapali 13, 20, 81, 84, 112, 116–23, 128, 148
Ananda 10, 74, 76, 89, 114, 124, 125
Anathapindika 56, 72–7, 81, 106, 109, 139
Angulimala 100, 108
Apadana 5, 30, 42, 44
apsara/s 15, 16, 20, 88, 149, 151, 161; *see also* acchara
Aramaic 15, 28, 29, 34, 35, 36, 39, 49
Aryan 19, 31, 162ff.
Aryavarta 2, 19
asava 50, 59, 60, 61, 63, 64, 66, 67, 69, 70, 146, 147
Ashoka 6, 9, 16, 17, 17n, 18, 21, 23–5, 26, 36, 44, 48, 95, 150–6, 158, 172, 173, 180, 181, 183, 185
asura 7, 14, 15, 26, 27, 33, 34, 35, 40, 41, 42, 48, 49, 164, 173, 174, 195
atavi 17, 21, 151, 172, 180
Avesta 32, 33n, 66

Bactria 9, 34, 35, 41, 66; *see also* Balhika
Balhika 35, 41; *see also* Bactria
Bhadatamahila 195
Bhadda 90, 141, 144
bhang/bhanga xiii, 57, 68, 69
Bharhut stupa 21, 45–7, 86–9, 104, 131, 156, 158–61, 165–80, 185–95
bhikkhu/s, bhikkhuni/s xiii, 10, 20, 21, 22, 24, 41, 51, 55, 56, 57, 58, 62, 63, 69, 77, 78, 80, 81, 82, 85, 86, 87, 89, 91, 95, 96, 98–103, 106, 107, 120, 124–5, 136, 139–42, 145–7, 154–6
bhutas 21, 23, 38, 153, 156, 193, 195
Bimbisara 22, 52–5, 84, 94–107, 110, 122, 128, 129, 131, 179, 184
Bodh Gaya 6, 42, 154, 183; *see also* Uruvela
bodhisatta/s 18

203

Brahmana 17, 97, 151, 158, 180
Brahmans 3, 16, 19, 33, 36–8, 40, 41, 48, 51, 59, 63–6, 70, 104–6, 135, 137, 139, 167, 186
Buddhaghosha 4

Cada Yakkhi 187, 189
Cakavako Nagaraja 188, 189, 192
caste 3, 7, 8, 11, 13, 38, 40, 48, 51, 52, 91, 118, 119, 126, 127, 139, 143, 148, 162, 169
Central Asia 2, 9, 31, 32, 35, 36, 42, 44, 49, 50, 64, 66, 67, 68, 161, 167
Chandalas 91, 162, 168, 170, 171
Chapadeva 156, 157
Citta 156, 157
courtesan 3, 13, 20, 21, 40, 52, 60, 61, 80, 81, 84, 85, 112, 118, 119, 121–3, 158, 167, 186

daha, dasa 173
Darius III 9, 27, 28, 34
Deccan 6, 23, 51, 94, 95, 115
deva/s 14, 15, 20, 22, 26, 33, 40–2, 48, 77–9, 82, 84, 90, 156, 158, 163–6, 172, 173, 186
Devadatta 101, 102, 113, 176, 177
Devata Culacoka 186, 188
devata/s 20, 22, 86, 87, 158, 186, 188
dhamma 17, 24, 75, 89, 114, 169, 183
Dhammadinna 139, 140, 144
Dhammapada 79
Digha Nikaya 6, 102

Erapata the Nagaraja 175

gahapati 7, 19, 48, 52, 71, 72, 89, 97, 106, 136, 138, 139, 145, 148, 167, 168
ganasangha 2, 6, 8, 10, 12, 52, 57, 71, 72, 94, 101, 102, 104, 105, 109, 110, 111, 114–19, 123, 124, 126–8, 138, 139
Gandara 9, 29, 30, 32, 34–9, 48–50, 69, 173
Gandhara 3, 4, 9, 67, 182
gandharva/s 15, 16, 149, 150
Ganges plain 2, 6, 8, 15, 18, 23, 26, 28, 37, 38, 48, 51, 67, 69, 100, 116, 128, 152
Gangito Yakho 188, 191
Gautama 65, 70; Four Noble Truths and 3, 40, 59, 73, 76, 92, 140

haoma 64, 66, 67; *see also* soma
Hellenistic 9, 16
Himalaya foothills 2, 8, 14, 38, 40, 66, 94, 104, 115, 117, 128
Hindu Kush 2, 34
Hindush 9, 29, 32, 35, 37, 50, 52, 173
Horse Sacrifice 14, 15, 149

Indo-European 14, 15, 19, 28, 31, 32, 34, 66, 143, 149, 171–3
Indus Valley 9, 19, 180
Isidasi 144

Jainas 16, 17, 141, 151
jataka/s 5, 18, 24, 37, 38, 107n, 109n, 110n, 115, 126n, 127, 131n, 132n, 134n, 135n, 151, 153, 170, 174, 189, 190, 192, 193

jati(s) 167, 168
Jetavana 56, 72–4, 76, 81, 89, 97, 106, 107, 109, 132, 134
Jivaka 21, 40, 48, 51–7, 70, 84, 95–7, 103, 145, 146, 163, 181

Kalinga 17, 151, 180
Kandahar 2, 9
Kapilavastu 10
Kasi 104, 107, 111, 131
Kassapa 91
Kattavahan 18
Khattiya 41, 109, 126, 127; *also see* Ksatriya
Khema 95, 96, 100, 128–31, 139, 146
kinnaras 7, 23, 24, 153
Kokaliya 177, 178n
Kosala, Koshala 2, 8, 10, 19, 53, 72, 73, 79, 94–6, 101, 104, 106, 108–11, 114, 117, 126–32, 184
Ksatriya 2, 8, 12, 65, 94, 105, 109, 111, 114, 118, 126, 167
Kubera 15, 16, 149, 150, 158, 164, 166, 172

Licchavis 8, 11–13, 111–13, 116–23

Magadha, Greater Magadha 2, 4–6, 8, 9, 11–13, 19, 21, 23, 38, 45, 48, 51, 52, 55, 72, 79, 94, 95, 97, 98, 102–4, 106, 110, 111, 113, 114, 117, 118, 122, 123, 128, 130, 131, 141, 153, 172, 180, 181, 184
Magadhi 4, 38, 171, 189
Mahabharata 18, 114

mahajanapadas 5
Mahakapi Jataka 174, 190, 191, 193
Mahavira 37, 112, 113, 119, 141
Mahayana Buddhism x, 59, 172, 179
Mallika 81, 106, 108, 109, 126, 130–6, 148
Mara 4, 158, 165, 166
Matanga Jataka 170
matrilineal communities 20, 21, 22, 84, 151, 152, 155
Mauryan Empire 6, 8, 9, 16, 23, 24, 29, 35, 36, 44, 48, 95, 122, 150, 152, 153, 172, 180, 181, 192
Missakesi 89, 161
Moggallana 20–2, 61, 78, 82, 89, 102, 103, 152, 154, 164, 166, 177, 178
Mucalinda 154

naga/s 7, 16, 21, 23, 24, 25n, 41, 42, 73, 121, 149, 150, 153–6, 166, 167, 172–7, 181, 182
nagaraja 154, 175–7, 188, 192
Nagarjuna 156, 172
Nagasena 156, 172
nibbana 61, 78, 121n, 140, 169; *see also* nirvana
niraya 175
nirvana 40, 77, 78, 121, 130, 140
nishadas 24

outcaste 38, 91, 122, 148, 163, 164, 178
Oxus 9

Pajapati, Maha Pajapati 9, 10, 81, 124–8, 139, 144–6
Pali Buddhist canon 3, 4
Pali Text Society 4, 5
Panini 19, 35, 38, 39, 41, 48
Pasenadi 79, 94–6, 104, 106–10, 126–35, 184, 185
Pataliputra 24, 153
Persepolis 9, 27n, 29, 30, 36, 42, 44
Persian Empire 9, 15, 26, 27, 29, 30, 32, 34, 42, 44, 47, 49, 69, 173; *see also* Achaemenid
peta 5, 22, 178, 179
Peta-Vatthu 21, 22, 178, 179
peti 22, 137, 178, 179
Prakrit 3, 6, 7, 29, 38, 50, 72, 171, 172
Prana Kassapa 168

Rhys Davids, T.W. 4, 8n, 10n, 21n, 59
raja, maharaja 3, 6, 10–12, 94, 111, 117–19, 122, 126–8, 130–2, 138, 145, 154, 164, 185
Rajagaha 6, 12, 20–2, 33, 40, 51–3, 63, 72, 73, 83, 84, 91, 95–8, 101, 102, 104, 109, 110, 114, 118, 122, 139, 148, 158, 184, 186; *see also* Rajagriha
Rajagriha xiv, 6
Rajjumala 92
rakshasa/s 15, 33, 41, 149

Sakka 20, 40, 78, 79, 82, 88–92, 158, 164
Sakya ganasangha 2, 10, 94, 101, 109, 110, 115, 117, 124
Sakyamuni 2, 9, 10, 20, 42, 94, 115, 125, 154, 175

Sakyas, Sakyans 2, 8, 9, 10, 19, 101, 104, 105, 109–11, 117, 124, 126–8, 136, 146, 154
Salavati 20, 21, 52, 84, 95, 122, 148
samana 97, 158; *see also* shramana
Samavati 136, 137, 144
Sambhuta 38, 39
Sanchi 21, 23, 24, 42–7, 152–6, 158, 161, 167, 172, 173, 177, 180–7, 195
sangha 3, 4, 5, 7, 8, 10, 12, 16, 20–3, 35, 40, 41, 51, 53, 55–8, 61–4, 66, 69–87, 89–110, 112–30, 132, 134, 137–47, 150–2, 155, 156, 172, 174, 176–9
Sanskrit Buddhist texts 4
Sariputta 19, 21, 22, 74, 76, 83, 89, 101–3, 141, 152, 154, 177, 179
Satapatha Brahmana 15n, 18, 20, 26, 33
satrap 28, 29, 34, 173
satrapy / satrapies 9, 26–30, 32, 35, 37, 50, 52, 67
Savatthi/Sravasti 6, 56, 72–4, 79, 81, 97, 106, 107, 127, 130, 132, 133, 142, 185
Seleucid Empire 9
Seleucus Nikator 9
setthi, shreshthi 71
Shakuntala 18, 20, 151
Shramana 151, 180; *see also* samana
Siddhartha 2
Sirima 21, 84–7, 90, 95, 158, 186
Soma 63–7, 70, 146
Subba 145
Subhadda 89, 90, 161
Suchiloma 100, 158, 159, 172, 187

INDEX

Sujata 75, 76, 134n, 178, 179
Sunga dynasty 23–5, 153, 156, 158, 172, 186
Susa 9, 30, 36

Taxila / Takshashila 2, 9, 15, 19, 21, 26–8, 30, 35–40, 48, 50–3, 56, 173
Theragatha 21n, 59, 152n
Theravada 3, 4
Therigatha 59, 61n, 96n, 118n, 129n, 136n, 140n, 141n, 144n
Thirteenth Edict 151
Thirty-three Devas 20, 78n, 164, 166, 173
Tibetan Buddhist 4

Ujjeni / Ujjayini, Ujjain 54, 55
Upaniṣads 26, 33, 163
Uposatha 23, 99, 104, 174
Uruvela 42, 43, 97, 154, 175; see also Bodh Gaya
Uttara 83–6

Vajji Ganasangha 8, 52, 57, 72, 94, 111, 116
Vajjian 12, 13, 112–14, 123
vanna, varna 168, 169
Varuna 163
Vassakara 12, 13, 114, 123
Vedic 14–16, 18–20, 26, 28, 33, 34, 38, 39, 42, 63, 64, 66, 67, 78, 104, 114, 135, 146, 148, 150, 151, 156, 163, 167, 172, 173

Vedisa / Vidisha 23, 24, 153, 155–8, 172, 182, 183, 185, 186, 193, 195
Vejayanta 164
Venavana 63, 95, 97, 100, 104
Vesali, Vaishali 6, 8, 10, 11–13, 20, 57, 61, 72, 81, 84, 94, 111–13, 116–24, 126, 128, 146, 148
Vidudabha 10, 109–11, 126–9, 133, 136
vihara/s 74, 82, 92
Vimanavatthu 5, 20, 78, 82n, 83, 84n, 85n, 86, 88–93, 160, 161n
Vinaya Pitaka 5, 10n, 40n, 52n, 53n, 58n, 68, 69, 72n, 79, 80n, 81n, 84n, 97n, 101n, 102n, 103n, 106n, 108n, 120n, 121n, 124n, 126n, 145n, 146n, 177n
Virudhaka Yakkho 187, 190
Visakha 71, 77, 79, 80, 81, 82, 86, 106, 107, 139
Visakha, husband of Dhammadinna 139, 140
Vulture's Peak 12, 97, 104, 114

Yakkha / Yakkhi, Yaksha / Yakshi 7, 16, 21, 23, 24, 33, 72, 73, 150, 153, 155, 156, 158, 164, 166, 167, 172, 174, 181, 182, 187, 189
Yama 163
Yavanas / Yonas 17, 49, 151

Zoroastrian 26, 27, 30–5, 37–9, 41, 42, 48–50, 64, 66–8, 173

www.ingramcontent.com/pod-product-compliance
Ingram Content Group UK Ltd.
Pitfield, Milton Keynes, MK11 3LW, UK
UKHW041938030225
454602UK00004B/410